REEL LATINXS

Latinx Pop Culture

SERIES EDITORS

Frederick Luis Aldama and Arturo J. Aldama

REEL LATINXS

Representation in U.S. Film and TV

Frederick Luis Aldama and Christopher González

THE UNIVERSITY OF
ARIZONA PRESS

TUCSON

The University of Arizona Press
www.uapress.arizona.edu

© 2019 by The Arizona Board of Regents
All rights reserved. Published 2019

ISBN-13: 978-0-8165-3958-1 (paper)

Cover design by Leigh McDonald
Cover art by J. Gonzo

Publication of this book is made possible in part by funding from subventions from
the College of Humanities and Social Sciences, Utah State University, and from the
Department of English, Utah State University.

Library of Congress Cataloging-in-Publication Data are available from the Library
of Congress.

Printed in the United States of America
♾ This paper meets the requirements of ANSI/NISO Z39.48-1992 (Permanence
of Paper).

For our *niñas*

CONTENTS

PREFACE

Latinx Pop Culture Matters

After each of us had spent years lecturing and writing on Latinx pop culture, we decided to sit down together and write a book on the subject. *Coco*'s smashing box-office records lit the fire. That Disney/Pixar finally reached beyond Speedy Gonzales comfort zones and actually hired Latinxs (after initial backlash when they *did not* consult Latinxs) to voice the characters; consult on the story, culture, and history; and assist with the film's helming was a watershed. And that the movie cleared upward of $740 million at the box office in the United States and abroad—spurred on by all the Latinx families in the United States and those in Mexico and South America who poured into theaters—showed the world that, indeed, the distillation and reconstruction of Latinx culture, experience, and subjectivity *mattered*. It was a win-win—for the corporate moneymakers and for us. Unfortunately, *Coco* is exceptional in this regard. And we think it's important to share with you the long history of why.

As this book will begin to lay out, the representation of Latinxs in mainstream television and film is not only plagued by willful misrepresentations but also is completely out of step with Latinx demographic presence in the United States. As our numbers have grown—and today we, the Latinxs of the United States, are steadfastly the majority minority with 50 million plus—this misrepresentation has become even more obvious and shameful. With Latinxs already the majority population in the Southwest and growing most abundantly in the South and Midwest, no matter where one lives today, one is bound to see, engage with, and even know a Latinx person. As Chris Rock said of the nearly all-white Oscars in 2016, you really have to go out of your way *not* to find a Latinx in L.A. So, in spite of what some have identified as the Browning of America, producers and creators in Hollywood and mainstream TV continue to either look the other way, deliberately erase us, or lazily turn their attention to stereotypes

Friz Freleng and Hawley Pratt's Speedy Gonzales created for Warner Brothers *Looney Tunes* and *Merrie Melodies* cartoon series

of yesteryear: from the malapropistic Speedy (whoever thought *arriba arriba* means "go go"?) to those banditos in Westerns and comic books to hypersexualized spitfire Latinas.

At the same time that we think a roadmap through the history of our *mis*representation is necessary, we also see within this history moments of rupture. Sometimes in the most unexpected places in mainstream TV and film, Latinx subjectivities have been reconstructed in complex ways. We think not only of some recent prime-time shows such as *Cristela* (2014–2015), *Superstore* (2015–), and the even more nuanced all-Latinx casted reboot of *One Day at a Time* (2017–2019), but also of shows such as *CHiPs* (1977–1983) and *Chico and the Man* (1974–1978). And so, while the general trajectory of Latinx representation has been one that nearly flatlines a simplistic and racist reconstruction of Latinx subjectivity and experience, there have been moments when we see a definite heartbeat, as we will examine throughout this book.

Before going any further, a quick word about our use of the term *Latinx*. For many decades, peoples in the United States who trace their roots to Latin America and have Spanish-speaking ancestors have struggled with an adequate and acceptable term of identity. *Latin, Hispanic, Spanish, Mexican American, Chicano, Latina/o, Latin@,* and many more identity terms have found their way into discussions of the exploration and expression of heritage. And all have, in some way, been found wanting. There is, therefore, no definitive term that satisfies everyone, as Suzanne Oboler has extensively observed. The most recent term for this community is *Latinx* (pronounced Latin-ex or LaTEEN-ex), with the *x* signifying a gender-neutral identity label that refrains from making an assumption about a person. The term began appearing on social media in 2014, and its usage has steadily grown (Salinas Jr. and Lozano, 1). We use the term throughout the book as a reminder of inclusivity and openness even though we recognize that not everyone is completely comfortable with the term and that many in the general public may not even understand yet what the term connotes. Conversely, not all scholars who work with any of the myriad of issues concerning this community accept the term *Latinx* unproblematically, if at all. Indeed, several scholars, including Richard T. Rodríguez, have written compellingly about the troubled nature of the term. Nevertheless, we believe the use of the term here, despite any shortcomings it may have, does the important work of signaling inclusivity. For us, the *x* also marks the wound of a shared colonized legacy of exploitation and oppression. We would like to state that we are aware of the ever-evolving nature of labels (per Oboler), and we take up the term with the knowledge that the *x*, as Rodríguez (203) notes, may cross out or omit something important to someone who may read this. We also considered varying the terms we use (i.e., *Latinx* sometimes, *Latino* other times), but deemed that doing so might only confuse readers. So, we have agreed on using *Latinx* and its variants throughout, and we welcome opinions to the contrary.

Finally, when writing this book, we envisioned it as a primer for our readers, and our tone and discussion is intended to be engaging and comprehensive. That is, we kept our respective scholarship along with that of our *colegas* in Latinx pop culture to an omnipresent whisper, though we have included "Further Reading" sections as an acknowledgment that our explorations of these topics are largely possible because of the scholarly work of many people. We have also included an extensive list of suggested readings and viewings of primary and secondary materials at the end of the book. We wrote the book in a language and form that are as accessible as possible, avoiding the sometimes impedimental academese and jargon. The inviting prose, however, does not signal a lack of rigorous engagement with these issues on our part. To this end, we organized the book into several main divisions that include smaller subdivisions identified by an italicized general statement. This allows us to move flexibly through a whole range of topics and primary texts *and* to keep to a clear argumentative path. With this we welcome you on this introductory journey through Latinx reels that matter deeply to Latinx real lives.

REEL LATINXS

INTRODUCTION

Real and Reel Latinx Lives Matter

I Want My MTV . . .

We begin with how we consume images of Latinxs in the twenty-first century. We no longer watch films on VHS on low-definition TVs. Latinxs are just as adaptable as any other group to emerging technologies, of course. We see this especially with the youngest generations. Today's youth consume content on their smartphones and iPads usually long before their parents. Family time in front of the boob tube is an entirely different activity now. If it does happen, it's usually to watch shows that have already been consumed individually. And this can lead to children wanting to see a show again precisely because it's family time—something that's also becoming less and less a reality today where smartphones, iPads, and the like are creating more and more atomized viewing experiences. Also, often it's the new generation who are teaching us, the older generation, how to find our way back to communal time.

This might sound a bit like two older Latinxs waxing nostalgic, but we have to be proactive about how media affects our lives. It's not that we should ignore it. Perhaps, however, we can use it to reassert and clear those spaces for communal interactions. There has to be intentionality in our TV- and film-viewing activities in terms of when to watch and with whom. Otherwise, we'll all end up like those families we see increasingly out to dinner, each in their own, atomized zone plugged into their smartphones.

Social Media and Boots on the Streets

Representation is a crucial aspect of any kind of marginalized community. We know that. If we leave it to others to determine how we are represented, and if we do next to nothing to put an end to such limited conceptions of who we are as Latinxs, then it's easy for others to assign our assent, as indicated by our silence. We've seen the push toward more representation—and specifically *better* representation that includes Latinxs in the process—with social media movements such as #OscarsSoWhite and #RepresentationMatters. These push-backs, as important as they are, should be seen as only the beginning. And, of course, with the history of mainstream cultural gatekeeping that's left us at the back door (at best), this is easier said than done.

Pounding on these gates has achieved some success. Important watchdog entities such as UnidosUS (formerly the National Council of La Raza [NCLR]) and the National Hispanic Media Coalition (NHMC) continue to do important work to wake the world to Latinx matters—media and other. NHMC, along with the Latinx community in L.A., protested the 2018 Oscars, first at the Oscars Nominee Luncheon, and then during the weekend of the Oscars. We need these boots on the streets. We need social media protests. We need programming put in the face of the world, like "New Voices," introduced at the 2018 Oscars by Ashley Judd, Annabella Sciorra, and Salma Hayek. We need enlightened African American directors such as Barry Jenkins, Ava DuVernay, and Lee Daniels and writers like Jordan Peele standing side by side with U.S. Latinx directors such Peter Bratt, Eddy Olmos, Alex Rivera, Aurora Guerrero, Patricia Cardoso, and many others. For systemic change we all need to stand in solidarity with other communities of color and with women.

Today more than ever advertisers understand the power of the Latinx demographic, and thus boycotts of shows, networks, or advertisers have the potential to effect change. More to the point, objections must be raised in a collective manner, or else it is assumed that Latinxs are perfectly okay with not being represented in film and TV. It is consistent pressure from these groups and from audiences that has helped make a difference and has led to many of the relative changes we now see when we tune in to a network's programming. Latinxs can make this change even more effective by supporting such organizations as NCLR, the Asociación de Empresarios Mexicanos (AEM), and NHMC. These groups are able to constantly point out the shortcomings of the TV programming we consume.

Digital Platforms and the Long Game

That's the long game, of course. In the meanwhile, we can create, and we are creating on multimodal venues and internet platforms with significant pathways to audiences. This was impossible not long ago. Before the advent of the internet it was incredibly difficult to make a film or TV show on one's own. There are notable luminaries. Among them is Robert Rodriguez, about whom we've both written extensively and comprehensively, who made on a shoestring ($7,000) what some might say is his most significant film: *El Mariachi* (1991). He spent on that film what some large Hollywood productions spend on lunch.

Although Robert was an exception, his just-do-it creative spirit was also prescient. Today, we're seeing more and more Latinx creators working with digital technology and internet distribution channels to get their stories out to thousands of viewers. We're going *rasquache*—that technique of making something worthwhile out of little to nothing at all—with our low-cost, high-tech audio-visual creations that burrow underneath and around fences and erstwhile-locked gates. Yesteryear's gatekeepers are losing control.

So we have someone like LeJuan James (#TeamLeJuan), who amassed a huge audience (1.5 million plus followers) for his day in the life of a Latinx episodes. Facebook, Twitter, YouTube, and Instagram, among others, have become digital media spaces for Latinx creators to get their stories out and, in each case, to potentially change tomorrow's narrative of Latinx identity and experience.

Just because a given Latinx narrative goes viral, though, doesn't mean that it's radically altering the social media landscape. There's a

El Mariachi (played by Carlos Gallardo) battling thugs in Robert Rodriguez's *El Mariachi* (1992)

difference between Kathy Cano-Murillo's blogging about her "Boho-Mex" (Craftychica.com) and a webisode of *East Willy B*. We can hear the hugely popular Latinx Tejeda Ruiz as the beauty vlogger Dulce Candy. There's nothing wrong with Cano-Murillo's and Ruiz's work. As homegrown celebrities with millions of followers, the corporate buy button at their sites provide them with a living. However, their work won't make audiences "woke" to the U.S. sociocultural and political landscape, which continues consistently to denigrate Latinxs. In both cases, the digital platforms and the internet lead to a wide circulation of Latinx narratives.

LATINX MARGINS HAVE THE POWER TO CHANGE MAINSTREAM CENTERS OF CULTURAL PRODUCTION

Internet and paid streaming platforms such as Hulu, Vevo, Twitch, Netflix, and Amazon Prime, among others, have changed the viewing habits of the general populace. Indeed, these streaming services compete directly with network and cable TV. And they've begun to radically alter the very content that's circulating for our consumption. Netflix and Amazon are now large enough to create their own filmic content; some of this content is so good it's competing for major film and TV awards. Netflix bested HBO for Emmy nominations for the first time in 2018. Having more formats for content creates more opportunity for diverse representation. A show like *East Los High* (2013–2017) might never have been green-lighted by a major network; it originated with CW and then moved to Hulu.

The Mindy Project (2012–2017), a Fox show starring a woman of color, actor Mindy Kaling, was canceled and later picked up by Hulu. These are potent reminders that the dynamics of traditional media formats have changed.

In the end, however, we must move forward with our eyes wide open. Hulu, Netflix, Vevo, and others might be spaces for Latinx voices and stories to emerge, but the bigger they get in terms of corporations and producers seeking the bottom line—profits—the more *like* the Hollywood and Network system they potentially can become. In other words, just because we have more opportunity for diverse representation does not mean that it is a matter of course. Diverse representation will not occur if these venues aren't actively looking for diverse voices. It won't happen if diverse writers and actors aren't

Camila Barrios (played by Vannessa Vasquez) as bisexual Latinx high school student in Hulu's *East Los High* (season 2, episode 1, July 9, 2014)

seeking to gain entry into the industry. Hence, there is the continued need for consciousness-raising through our scholarship, teaching, and boots-on-the-ground activism.

THE DECLINE OF PRIME-TIME TV AND NEW WAYS TO CREATE AND DISTRIBUTE REEL LATINXS

What we're describing is the new reality of film and media consumption. Netflix, Hulu, Amazon Prime, and other streaming apps have recognized that there are very busy people who have to consume their viewing material on the go and when they can. The portability of our streaming devices and apps is tailor-made for this; it's actually easy to catch a little bit of a show at a coffee shop or in a doctor's waiting room. The days of sitting in front of a TV at the appropriate hour is really going the way of the T. rex, with the notable exception of live events such as sports. And even these can be streamed on the go.

Like so many today, we both binge-watch shows. We no longer identify a time and day when we might gather as a family to watch a TV program. Instead, we block off hours (sometimes late at night when the tykes are asleep) to consume huge quantities of a given plot and narrative. In this sense, too, the way serialized TV used to work is also a thing of the past. Netflix and Amazon Prime, in a brilliant move, decided to premiere not just a new show or new season one episode

Introduction

7

at a time but the entire season at once. Creators working with streaming platforms (and this includes networks such as CBS, with its paid streaming of *Star Trek: Discovery*) are making shows with complex, hugely expansive narrative arcs. Knowing the way our short-term and long-term memory works when consuming narratives, creators of shows such as *Luke Cage* or *Star Trek: Discovery* are apparently assuming they are appealing to an audience of binge-watchers.

Claire Temple (played by Rosario Dawson) in the Netflix series *Daredevil* (season 2, episode 3, 2016)

Of course, this also assumes their audience is of a certain socioeconomic status. Those working two, three, even four jobs to pay rent and put food on the table aren't worried about what happens next to the Latinx character Claire Temple (Rosario Dawson) in the Netflix series *Daredevil*; nor for that matter will they be surfing the net for links to extra-textual sites, such as social media fan sites.

CREATING SIMPLISTIC, CARELESS, AND DOWNRIGHT LAZY REPRESENTATIONS OF LATINXS

This simplification comes from laziness in storytelling and research. (This is something Frederick identifies as a lack of a *will to style* in his other work.) Today it's arguably even more than being lazy. It's downright racist. It doesn't take Chris Rock to tell us that it's hard *not* to find a Latinx person in L.A. to consult, write, or even work behind or in front of a camera. So when the world is complexly layered with Latinx peoples and yet the main prime-time Latinx figure today continues to be a hypersexualized, bumbling buffoon (Sofía Vergara as Gloria in *Modern Family*), and with little else to see and reflect on, then we can justify our position that this is racism.

An equally pernicious idea exists below the surface in the creation of all mainstream cultural phenomena: since these are the types of characters audiences want to see, this is what we'll continue to churn out. Capitalism works first to heterogenize, then to homogenize. Put simply, its first impulse is to diversify by throwing out as many cultural objects as possible, and then the one that sells becomes the one that's backed and promoted and reproduced ad infinitum until it no longer sells. The TV and film industries operate within this system—a global system. As wrong as it gets Latinxs and LGBTQ families, *Modern Family* continues to capture fourteen to eighteen million middle- and upper-middle-class viewers. That's fourteen to eighteen million wallets ready to open for goods advertised both in the show and during its plenitude of fifteen-to-thirty-second spots. No captain of the megalithic TV industry is going to mess with these numbers.

Because mainstream TV and film companies want to generate profit, they'll continue to churn out the same old narrative lite, even replicating the same characters and formulas in all their programming. Hence, all the clones and knockoffs.

It's important to bring to the fore, here, that many of us are *not* willing to be spoon-fed garbage. We want more: complexity, diversity, creativity. And these same hungry audiences are in some cases also writers and directors. Even with more formulaic narratives, we're seeing some great narrative innovation: from "new" *Alien* prequels and sequels to the *Star Wars* and *Star Trek* sagas, to reboots of *Hawaii Five-0* (2010–2018), *Lethal Weapon* (2016–), *Star Trek: Discovery* (2017–), and more. These industries like to go to the well of success in an attempt to recapture some of that magic, and often they are successful.

MEASURING DIVERSITY WHEN IT BECOMES SUCCESS

We've seen success in film and TV shows when diverse voices and identities are represented on the screen. And success—that is, profitability—matters most in these cases. Consider Disney's recent batch of *Star Wars* movies: *The Force Awakens* (2015), *Rogue One* (2016), and *The Last Jedi* (2017). Each of these films has been a box-office monster, both domestically and globally. But what makes this more exciting is that prominently featured actors from the gender and racial margins appear front and center in these films: Black Brit John Boyega, Guatemalan Latinx Oscar Isaac, Mexican Diego Luna, and Daisy Ridley, the first female lead in any *Star Wars* film—with Felicity Jones as costar (*Rogue One*).

Asian Americans also feature significantly in both *Rogue One* and *The Last Jedi*. These films have exposed audiences to diverse representation in this particular movie universe, and most, though

Poe Dameron (played by Oscar Isaac) in *Star Wars: The Force Awakens* (2015)

not all, have been enthusiastic about such casting and scripting decisions.

We mentioned that audiences don't passively sit back for spoon-feeding. Well, that cuts both ways. Radical, extremist, white-supremacist alt-right, and other movements spit these films back out, declaring them acts of "white genocide" and using social media to boycott them. In the end, however, this did little to put a dent in *Star Wars* reaching audiences across the world—and in the multimillions.

It might be that Disney is showing the rest of corporate media in the United States the way forward. It's worth remarking again that the meticulously researched and Latinx casted *Coco* (after initial backlash during development) killed it at the box office. That they brought on Latinx political cartoonist and noted Disney critic Lalo Alcaraz as a consultant is a near miracle by mainstream Hollywood standards. Back in 2014, when Disney tried to trademark the phrase "Day of the Dead" (the original name of the film), Alcaraz pushed back with his political cartoons, especially with his Godzilla-like "Muerto Mouse."

This caught their attention. Instead of blacklisting Alcaraz, they played it smart: they hired him as an advisor to the creative team to be sure they were getting the Mexican cultural elements of the story—the whole story actually—right.

Coco was a film of its time. It will become increasingly clear as one reads through this book that Thanksgiving weekend 2017, when Disney released *Coco*, marked a watershed in the mainstream's reel reconstruction of real Latinxs. That was a moment in U.S. mainstream media history when the cast and subject were completely of Mexican Latinx origin. Add to this the fact that it was an unmitigated financial and critical success, and we had a film that made history.

As we write this, it's still too early to tell, but we do see a ripple effect, or what we might call a *Coco* effect with *Black Panther* (2018),

Lalo Alcaraz's "Muerto Mouse" cover art for *OC Weekly* (October 2013)

and we are hopeful that that film will do what *Coco* did for superheroes of color in the Marvel and DC film universes.

LATINXS WATCH MORE TV AND GO TO THE MOVIES MORE THAN ANY OTHER U.S. DEMOGRAPHIC

Nielsen counts forty-eight million U.S. Latinxs watching TV at any given time. This doesn't include the millions consuming shows via their smartphones and streaming apps. We can add to this the fact that Latinxs make up one of the most reliable and largest blocks of moviegoers.

Latinxs are shelling out the bucks to watch films in the multiplex—and to buy all those tie-in tees, toys, lightsabers, Legos, and more.

We both can recall those days in the late 1970s after *Star Wars* stunned the world and when parents and children clamored for its toys in stores and for those McDonald's Happy Meals. We also remember that there weren't any Latinxs anywhere in sight, action figures or otherwise; the closest we could get was Lando after the 1980s release of *The Empire Strikes Back*. While our Latinx demographics weren't what they are today—we floated somewhere around the middle teens during the seventies and eighties—we still represented a buying demographic, one clearly ignored by the original *Star Wars* trilogy.

We know that the film and TV industries are run by the bottom line: profits. Yet it took decades before they realized Latinxs were a demographic with big purchasing power. We're not necessarily saying that creating Latinx characters in these early *Star Wars* films should have happened *because* of our purchasing power. It should have happened because we *exist* everywhere and therefore should be reconstructed in stories everywhere. What we are pointing out is the fact that it makes money sense to have us as part of *all* storytelling because, well, it'll generate more money for industry executives.

That producers are still absenting us from the mainstream clearly indicates that they are not ready to do the hard work of due diligence in order to ensure they avoid offensive stereotypes and make things worse by representing Latinxs in their storytelling in ways that alienate audiences. Yet every time there is a Latinx success—a major success in the industry—watch everyone want a piece of the action.

Consider Lin-Manuel Miranda. He wrote the lyrics and music and starred in his musical *In the Heights*, which put him on the map in the world of Broadway. That led him to sign on to write the music for Disney's *Moana*. At the same time he was writing what would turn out to be one the biggest musical hits in years—*Hamilton*. That musical, inspired by the "ten-dollar Founding Father," became a phenomenon, and even people who don't normally know much about musicals have heard of it. As a result, Miranda's exposure has grown, his star continues to rise, and he has appeared in the revamped animated series *DuckTales* (2017–) and in *Mary Poppins Returns* (2018). His talent is unquestionable. But it was his overwhelming critical and financial success that turned heads. Now, consider his basic premise for *Hamil-*

ton: a musical about the nation's first treasury secretary killed in a duel with Aaron Burr. It doesn't exactly sound as interesting as it actually is. But Miranda went a step further with the pathbreaking idea that all Founding Fathers and the women in their lives would be played not as the white men and women they were but as people of color. By disregarding that one inconvenient fact, the stories we thought we knew were elevated and reconfigured in our brains so that it was as if we were all seeing and hearing them for the first time. Miranda is a good example of putting money on quality. And because he identifies as a Latinx (he is Puerto Rican), producers and executives don't fear appropriation the way they would if they had come up with the idea. Executives are surely looking for the next Lin-Manuel Miranda.

The Anxiety of Arriving

Dora the Explorer (Nickelodeon, 2000–) has been teaching kids across the nation for nearly two decades. Latinx actors are cast as characters in galaxies far, far away. Television shows like *Jane the Virgin* (2014–) have nearly all-Latinx casts. *Coco* picked up the 2018 Oscar for Best Animated Feature, with its lead director Lee Unkrich (not Latinx co-director Adrian Molina) giving a shout-out to "the people of Mexico," stating that the film "would not exist without your endlessly beautiful culture and traditions" and concluding, "Representation matters."

Some might argue that Latinx representation is here, and so what are we complaining about. We know better. We still appear in less than 3 percent of all media, and this includes children's books, young-adult fiction, TV, film, and all else. Considering the difference between our 18 percent demographics and what we see in mainstream culture, we're clearly a long way from having arrived.

Now, if we had the Latinx equivalent of Marvel's *Black Panther* (film and comic), where the mainstream is seen, experienced, imagined, felt, and thought as brown, then, yes, we could talk about having arrived. But this raises another interesting element—anxiety. Hypothetically speaking, would we be somewhat anxious if by some *milagro* mainstream culture flipped things upside down and had whiteness swept aside and ignored? Consider the viral Facebook video that featured a black man in awe, standing in front of the *Black Panther* poster, who said, "Is this what white people feel all the time?!"

Introduction

13

Yes, that *Black Panther* has a nearly all black cast, director, and writers is remarkable. But it's still an anomaly. Our African American compadres aren't anxious about their arrival here. And we're not even close to this with Latinx superhero films—or any other films for that matter. So it's a little premature to talk about an *anxiety of arrival*.

That said, if arriving means whitewashing Latinx cultures and identities, as seen in Latinx Demi Lovato's Disney era of acting (*Camp Rock* and the like), or *Dora the Explorer*'s idea of Spanish use as only a tool without cultural content, then we'll take a pass. Arriving will be TV and film where all variety of Latinx culture and identities exist in richly resonant ways. We're far from this. And, so, we continue to critique and call out wherever necessary.

RECOGNITION OF LATINX FILM AND TV TALENT

Certainly, we should celebrate the fact that *Ugly Betty* picked up two Golden Globes, a SAG award, three Emmy awards, and the Gay and Lesbian Alliance Against Defamation award, among others. *Jane the Virgin* earned its fair share, with a Peabody, a Golden Globe, and a People's Choice award. But when it comes to films, it's not so bright and cheery.

With the exception of only one U.S. Latinx (Puerto Rican–born José Ferrer), we've been pretty much totally left out of the Oscars every year since they were founded in 1927. As a result, we've had to create our own institutions to recognize our achievements. We now have the American Latino Media Arts (ALMA) Award (created by the National Council of La Raza), the National Hispanic Foundation for the Arts, and the Hispanic Organization of Latin Actors (HOLA). These sorts of culturally specific awards provide an impetus for actors, artists, writers, and other creators to continue (or to begin) the important work of creating Latinx-infused art and stories.

Many academics have analyzed the significance of awards and their ceremonies as forms of ritualized theater. (See Jim English's *The Economy of Prestige*, for instance.) While this is certainly true, they do have material consequences for creators. If doors to the Oscars, the Golden Globes, and the Emmys are never open to Latinx creators, not only will Latinxs never be celebrated for their hard-earned accomplishments, but they will never reap the material benefits that accrue from such recognition.

It's important to make a distinction between U.S. Latinx creators and those south of the proverbial Tortilla Curtain, such as Alejandro González Iñárritu, Alfonso Cuarón, and Guillermo del Toro. All have picked up significant mainstream film awards. Iñárritu won Oscars for *Birdman* (2004) and *The Revenant* (2015). Cuarón won for *Gravity* (2013). Del Toro picked up a Golden Globe and an Oscar for Best Picture and Best Director for *The Shape of Water* at the 2018 awards. However, these films have nothing to do with U.S. Latinxs or Mexican Latinxs or Latinidad anywhere on the planet for that matter. They are innovative triumphs, and that we should celebrate. They show the world that the film narrative doesn't have to slip into the formulaic. And by not choosing to focus on what's expected—Mexican characters and content—they trouble the usual misguided idea that just because you're Latinx you should only create Latinx characters and subjects. Whether U.S. Latinx or from south of the border, we can and should create stories about everything and anything. We can also look here for inspiration from Japanese Swedish American director Cary Joji Fukunaga (whose father was born in a Japanese American internment camp), who made a beautiful and harrowing film called *Sin nombre* (2009), which is entirely in Spanish and set almost entirely in

Willy "El Casper" (played by Edgar Flores) with Lil Mago (played by Tenoch Huerta Mejía) in *Sin nombre* (2009)

Mexico. He then turned right around and made *Jane Eyre* and *Beasts of No Nation*, directed the critically acclaimed first season of the HBO smash *True Detective*, and adapted the screenplay for Stephen King's novel *IT*, another box-office success.

As the industry and audiences continue to recognize excellence in Latinx arts, we should remain cautious about the ways that Latinx creators are codified, pigeonholed, and mainstream-celebrated. Until we have U.S. Latinx creators on the same footing as other Latinxs such as del Toro et al., we can't really talk about Latinx in a panoramic or pan-Latinx way. We should celebrate our Mexican Latinx *compadres* but not confuse this with the "arriving" of Latinx film creators.

Latinxs Mainstreamed and the #MeToo Movement

We should question the kind of attention we receive. All too often it's the hypersexualized, business-as-usual kind of attention. Benjamin Bratt in a wet T-shirt on the cover of *Vanity Fair*; Gina Rodriguez

Jo Raquel Tejada as high school senior, winning San Diego County's "Fairest of the Fair" in 1958

pushing her cleavage into readers' faces in *Latina* magazine; and Jessica Alba's covers for *GQ* (June 2008), *In Style* (June 2008), *Playboy* (March 2006), and *Maxim*, in which she wasn't the girl next door. The target audiences for most of these publications are young, white men salivating and more over the exotic Other.

All this perpetuates a history of Latinas becoming sexual objects right before the public's eyes. Rita Hayworth (née Margarita Carmen Cansino) and Raquel Welch (née Jo Raquel Tejada) really established the Latina bombshell in Hollywood—a tradition that has continued with Salma Hayek, Jennifer Lopez, Patricia Ray, Sofía Vergara, Eva Longoria, and Jessica Alba.

All of these women have been sexualized in visual media. We love that Latinas are celebrated in the media. We'd also love to see more *types* of Latinas represented—all sexualities, body shapes, and skin-shade variations. We have Latinas who look like Jessica Alba, but also like Michelle Rodriguez. We have Latinos who look like Marc Anthony and Ricky Martin as well as those who look like George Lopez and *out* Orlando Cruz and Wilson Cruz.

Latinxs don't fit easily the narrow conceptions and expectations that have dictated what Latinxs look and act like on our movie and TV screens. Cameron Diaz smashes the stereotype of what a Latina looks like. A fair-skinned, blond-haired, blue-eyed woman, she has caused much consternation in audiences who either conveniently "forget" that her surname is Diaz or stubbornly refuse to acknowledge that she is Latina. The ethnicity of NFL pro quarterback (now retired) Tony Romo (né Antonio Ramíro Romo) is only sparingly referenced when he is mentioned. It's perfectly fine if Latinxs like Diaz and Romo don't wear their Latinidad on their sleeves or fit the expected "look" for a Latinx in the United States. But it is paramount that they be recognized as belonging to the Latinx community for the sole reason that doing so helps break that stubborn mold of expectation that people have when conceiving of what Latinxs look like, what they sound like, what they do for a living. All of this is necessary if stereotypes and caricatures are to be dismantled.

We, the Latinx writers of this book, defy many people's expectations for Latinxs. The two of us represent a diverse range: Frederick is fair skinned and speaks English perfectly without any hint of a Spanish accent. Christopher, a fifth-generation Texan, is brown skinned, but at six feet, three inches and over 250 pounds, he doesn't fit the narrow expectations for recently arrived Mexican American men. The media has us pegged as short and small, ill equipped to speak English. In fact, José Vasconcelos calls Latinxs "The Fifth Race" precisely because we don't fit within long-established molds. Today the term and Vasconcelos himself are problematic for many reasons, but his idea that Latinxs seems to be inclusive of all races does make a lot of sense. It is best to think of Latinxs as being variable when it comes to phenotype.

Linguistic variation among Latinxs is huge. Latinxs in the United States not only come in all shades, shapes, and sizes, but they also come with differing linguistic abilities. They run the gamut from strictly Spanish speaking to different degrees of bilingual proficiency to mostly, if not all, English speaking. Also, many of these mostly English-speaking Latinxs still are steeped in their culture. You have heritage speakers, or those Latinxs who understand Spanish but are not fluent in their speaking ability—so-called receptive bilingualism. Melissa Lozada-Oliva has a poem titled "My Spanish" in her book of poetry *Peluda* that has a poignant line that refers to this: "If you ask me if I'm fluent in Spanish, I will tell you my Spanish is an itchy phantom limb. It is reaching for words, and only finding air." To think of a language that is a part of your family's history and heritage and to then find you don't really have access to it makes one think of having lost something. But rather than dwell on this as a negative, why not accept the reality that Latinxs aren't *only* defined by their fluency in Spanish? There's a scene in *Blood In, Blood Out* (1993) when the character Montana (Enrique Castillo) tells the young, light-skinned protagonist Miklo (Damian Chapa), who is attempting to gain Montana's favor by speaking Spanish, "You speak Spanish, *güero*. So do parrots." It's the idea that being Latinx is more than just speaking a certain language in a certain way.

No matter our massive variety as a people, we're generally mainstreamed into the hypersexual and exotic. When Latinxs are dressed up for photo ops in wet tees, button-down shirts for full cleavage, it's the straight, white male gaze that seems be the one lensing and framing Latinas. No matter the skin complexion, linguistic cadence, or body shape, one way or another they continue to be hypersexualized and exoticized. This has material, everyday consequences. Some scholars have linked this white optic to the ways state- and industry-sponsored policies have justified the sterilization of Latinas. Seen only as objects and not human subjects, all sorts of officially sanctioned violence has been directed at Latinas.

Artists and scholars who are women of color have been critical of this *and* the color blindness of the feminist movement. We agree wholeheartedly with the #MeToo movement—there needs to be an awareness of histories of violence against women, the erasure of pay gaps, and equality on every single level of human existence. We also agree that racism and homophobia continue to pervade every level of society. Until we truly live in a postrace world, we will need solidarity across racial and sexuality divides to really push the #MeToo movement forward. Mainstream glossy mags with a select few flavor-of-the-month Latinas won't do this. So, yes, this mainstreaming produces a kind of prominence and visibility, but it comes at the cost of dignity and equal consideration for all genders and gender-neutral people.

Cultural Slumming, Brownface, and More

In F. Scott Fitzgerald's *The Great Gatsby* (1925), it's okay for Gatsby to be tanned from leisure activities—boating, tennis, and the like. But it's not okay to be tanned from labor in the sun. There was a moment in our recent history when white privilege paraded itself as such with tans from leisure activities—in which case one could justify transgression of social taboos. It became a way of crossing the border, like we see when Sal Paradise in Jack Kerouac's *On the Road* (1957) crosses into Mexico, temporarily goes "native," has a grand epiphany, then returns to his white privilege. Visit Cancun or Rosarita Beach during spring break and you'll see our twenty-first-century version of this.

And there's the case of Rachel Dolezel, the white woman born and raised as such who began to pass herself off as black. We see this with fraternities and sororities during Halloween: ponchos, mustachios, and skeletons all come out and adorn white privilege. These brownface performances inure the privileged into thinking it's not so bad to be dispossessed, to be disenfranchised. It's all wrapped in the gauze of entertainment in the service of a good time. Yet it is only a good time for some, not all.

These are cases of "cultural slumming." They are also instances of brownface—white folks assuming caricatured cultural characteristics of racially Othered peoples. Believe it or not, this continues to happen in film and TV. It was Robin Williams—and not, say, a Michael Peña—who was voicecast to play Ramon in *Happy Feet 2*. Whether a spring breaker, Dolezel, or Robin Williams, slumming it by performing brownface (or blackface) is a choice and not an everyday fact of life. While some like Jessica Alba might be able to pass as white, Latinxs and our African American and Asian brothers and sisters can't wash off our race or ethnicity, which is more than a temporary costume or fake accent.

This is what we mean when we differentiate between the haves and have-nots. What is for one group an inescapable reality is for another whimsy.

The 1980s as the Decade of the Hispanic

An October 1978 cover of *Time* magazine announced the 1980s as "The Hispanic Decade!" Indeed, it was an era when Latinx films seemed to pour through the floodgates: *Cheech and Chong's Next Movie* (1980), *Zoot Suit* (1981), Robert M. Young's *Ballad of Gregorio Cortez* (1982), *El Norte* (1985), *La Bamba* (1987), Gregory Nava's *El Norte* (1984), and Cheech Marin's *Born in East L.A.* (1987), to mention a few. It was also a moment when we began to see Latinx actors like Eddy Olmos in other film and televisual spaces like *Miami Vice* (1984–1989). Latinxs suddenly were to be imagined and seen in the future, with Olmos as Eduardo Gaff in *Blade Runner* (1982) and María Conchita Alonso as Amber Mendez in *The Running Man* (1987).

Given the small number of Latinx actors that appeared during the decades before, the eighties did seem like a watershed. But if we consider these within the eighties blockbuster filmscape, it's a drop in the bucket. There are no Latinxs in *The Empire Strikes Back* (1980), *Raiders of the Lost Ark* (1981), *E.T. the Extra-Terrestrial* (1982), *Back to the Future* (1985), *The Breakfast Club* (1985), and all other eighties blockbuster films, unless we count Spanish-descended Brit Alfred Molina's small scene in the opening of *Raiders of the Lost Ark*.

The early twenty-first century feels different from what came before not just in quantity but also in content. Latinx films of the 1980s were very niche—and for good reason. Directors wanted to get our

Satipo (played by Alfred Molina) in *Raiders of the Lost Ark* (1981)

histories, experiences, and stories out to the public for mass consumption. *Zoot Suit, La Bamba*, and *The Ballad of Gregorio Cortez* are all rooted in biographical or historical events. They are "slice of Latinx life" films that capture Latinxs in their natural environs as if they were anthropological documentaries. By contrast, see how few instances of Latinxs in nonbiographical or nonhistorical films there were as the twentieth century began to draw to a close.

The Latinx 1990s

In the 1990s, we began to see greater range of Latinx content and across all variety of genres: *El Mariachi* (1992), *American Me* (1992), *Mi vida loca* (1993), *I Like It Like That* (1994), *A Million to Juan* (1994), *Mi familia* (1995), *Desperado* (1995), *Selena* (1997), among others. These and other Latinx-centric films were bankrolled and distributed by major Hollywood players tacking in a new direction. Like many Latinx audiences, we jumped for joy. We shelled out our hard-earned pesos to see ourselves (and relatable yet radically different versions of ourselves) on the silver screen. But, like the 1980s, these were still a drop in the bucket compared with the wave of mainstream block-busters that featured the usual white-savior tropes, for example, films such as *Jurassic Park* (1993), *Armageddon* (1998), and the like. Even in a film such as *Independence Day* (1996)—which features a black character, Captain Steve Hiller (played by Will Smith)—it's the white, alcoholic ex-fighter pilot Russell Casse (played by Randy Quaid) who saves the day—and the planet.

Countering the continued white saturation at the multiplex during this time, Univision and Telemundo were streaming Spanish-language shows right into our *salas*. Latinx families could tune into shows such as *El Chapulín Colorado* and *El Chavo del Ocho*, both masterminded by Roberto Gómez Bolaños, who played the role of "Chespirito" in *El Chavo* and the title role in *El Chapulín*. These and Mexican comedy films from the seventies such as *La India María* and *¡Ahi, madre!* filled an all too real void in Hollywood films and major network shows for many Latinxs in the United States, even in rerun broadcasts as the millennium approached.

This phenomenon was the beginning of a growing trend: Latinxs consuming more and more Spanish-language media, and not just among our *abuelos y abuelas*. Today, Telemundo's bilingual

Chespirito (played by Roberto Gómez Bolaños) in *El Chapulín Colorado* (1973–1979)

programming network, Mun2, reaches over forty million homes. And there is all sorts of other Latinx programming in the offing in the first few decades of the twenty-first century. In 2013, Robert Rodriguez won the contract with Comcast to launch the El Rey network—and he did so partly in a pitch that talked precisely about the need for Latinx programming in English. But there are other programing offerings, such as Nuvo (with Jennifer Lopez as creative officer and a major stakeholder) as well as Fusion (Univision and Disney Co.), seeking to grab Latinx millennials who are bilingual or even mostly English speaking. All of these endeavors remind the media world that Latinx audiences crave stories created by and for Latinxs, that we want to be in front of the camera and behind it, and that our hemispheric cultures, identities, and experiences *across* languages matter.

Using and Troubling the Latinx Category

"Latinx" is a category that includes U.S. Latinos and Latinas from Mexican, Central American, South American, and hispanophone Caribbean ancestry and heritage. It is a vast group that no single term can accurately encompass. And while such an umbrella category has its shortcomings—it can erase important differences between our different cultures, sociopolitical histories, and the like—we see it as important for bringing together all Latinxs in a unified front.

For the purposes of some things such as the U.S. census, having one term for all individuals with a Spanish-speaking ancestor or from a Latin American country increases that particular demographic bloc and with it increased federal and state funding for resources. If we start slicing and dicing the Latinx category, then the collective bargaining power the term *Latinx* once held is gone, and in its place there are many smaller groups. Mexican Americans, the largest bloc of Latinxs in the United States, would be hurt relatively less than, say, Dominican Americans or Uruguayan Americans. These smaller subdemographics, already a portion of a minority, would suddenly become an even smaller minority in the United States. In this case, the utilitarian aspect of the term *Latinx* mitigates the homogenization it produces.

When it comes to film and TV, however, we should strive to make sure there are plentiful examples of parity and diversity in Latinx representation. Actually, it seems we might be marching in the right direction. Today we have more Latinx subgroups represented in Hollywood and on Broadway than we did in the 1980s and 1990s—an epoch dominated by Mexican American and Cuban American representation.

CASTING LATINX ACTORS

Puerto Rican Latinx Esai Morales made his claim to fame cast in Chicano roles—in *La Bamba, Zoot Suit*, and *Mi Familia*, for instance. Peruvian and Anglo (German, English, Austrian) Benjamin Bratt has played Nuyoricans, such as Miguel Piñero, and Chicano gangbangers.

Roberto "Bob" Morales (played by Esai Morales) in *La Bamba* (1987)

Of Surinamese and Puerto Rican ancestry, Jimmy Smits has played every kind of Latinx under the sun. Puerto Rican/Dominican Latina Zoe Saldana (née Zoe Yadira Saldaña Nazario) is often cast as African American, such as in the rebooted *Star Trek* film franchise, or as alien in James Cameron's *Avatar* (2009). America Ferrera, who is of Honduran Latinx ancestry, was cast as a Mexican Latinx in *Ugly Betty*. The trend continues with Gina Rodriguez, who is of Puerto Rican descent, playing the Mexican Latinx in *Jane the Virgin*.

In a perfect media world, the respective percentages of all Latinx demographic groups and subgroups would be represented; there would be a perfect synchronization between society and the actors, producers, filmmakers, directors, and so on. Imagine a situation in which the Mexican American demographic in roles on the screen matched perfectly the Mexican American demographic in society. So far that sounds too good to be true—and perhaps it is. However, if in this perfect scenario we found that Mexican American actors were playing only Mexican American roles, at some point we would probably say, "Wait! Mexican American actors can play more than just Mexican American characters! We're stifling them by having them play only to their ethnicity!"

While many roles are written with specific ethnicity markers in mind, many characters are written without considering ethnicity or race. And while it's certainly not a perfect situation when we have Ferrera cast as a Latinx of Mexican descent or when Cuban Americans portray Nuyorican American characters, it is still preferable to Hollywood's long and continuing history of whitewashing.

We want parity in opportunity for all groups, not just Latinxs. And, ultimately, we should be striving for a silver screen and televisual landscape that's neither tokenizing nor proscriptive. Until we have total parity—until we live in a postrace society globally—the same goal should apply to all casting, but until then it's important that a director choose not to cast, for instance, an Idris Elba or John Boyega as black American men or, for that matter, cast an African American actor to play a blatino character, as Barry Jenkins did in the otherwise masterful *Moonlight*. But the material fact remains that today actors of color have to live and so must take roles they are offered.

It's also true that no matter whether actors with Latinx ancestry align with the roles played—think Michael Peña, who plays Mexican

Angie (played by Constance Marie) and George (played by George Lopez) in *George Lopez* (season 6, episode 1, 2013)

Latinx Poncho in the film *CHiPs* or George Lopez in *The George Lopez Show* (2001–2007) and his semiautobiographical *Lopez*—because of the paucity of Latinx roles and representations in the media, they suddenly stand in for *all* Latinxs. Scholar and Pulitzer Prize–winner Viet Thanh Nguyen has coined the term *narrative plentitude* to highlight the fact that the dominant white culture has so many narratives, it can afford to have what might be disastrous or stereotypical turns when applied to marginalized cultures who would have, per Nguyen, what we might call "narrative scarcity." Those who can, like George Lopez, end up simultaneously entertaining and educating audiences about the different cultural, historical, and socioeconomic circumstances that differently shape the Latinx identity and experience of a Mexican (George Lopez) and two Cubans (his wife, Angie, played by Constance Marie, and her father Vic). (We also see this in *Blackish*.) But it requires more opportunities to shape societal understandings of less represented cultures.

Put another way, what George Lopez does—and is expected to do—is very different from what Jerry Seinfeld does and is expected to do in *Seinfeld*. Jerry never has to explain his specific cultural or historical circumstances to his audience, and yet we as the audience learn what we need to in order to make the show work. Shows such as *Cristela* and *The George Lopez Show* are obligated to educate an audience outside of the Latinx cultural sphere—a manifestation of how whiteness (even white Jewishness) is *normative* and brownness Othered. This phenomenon is narrative scarcity made visible.

JANITORS, MALINCHES, AND BUFFOONS

Though *Will and Grace* (1998–2006) made headlines for its depictions of gay characters, it certainly didn't earn points for its representation of Latinxs, which consisted of a brief appearance of a maid. Cheech Marin as Joe Dominguez in *Nash Bridges* (1996–2001) basically played the role of sidekick and cleanup crew to an Anglo protagonist (Don Johnson). In ABCs *Gideon's Crossing* (2000–2001) Max Cabrenas's sole purpose seemed to be to offer empathic support to emotionally overwrought Anglos. And with Wilmer Valderrama's character Fez in *That '70s Show* (1998–2006), we saw only a slight makeover of the oversexed buffoon stereotype. The thickly Spanish-accented Rico appeared only to serve as sounding board to all varieties of racialized and sexualized jokes in *King of Queens* (1998–2007). And it's the Latinx character Natalie in *Felicity* (1998–2002) who plays the double-crossing malinche figure doing whatever it takes to get what she wants. All of these characters embody the limited experience, due diligence, and imagination of the writers who created them. They must never have imagined that the character Nash Bridges could have just as easily been a Latinx cop with a white sidekick who cleaned up all the messes. The only thing that prevents the creation of such a character is the inability to imagine it. If we are being kind to the writers and assume that they sometimes attempt to go against the tradition of the cardboard cutout Latinx, then blame falls to the producers, showrunners, or executives who green-light shows. Yet we are again at the bleeding edge of this trend if we consider the 2018 reboot of the 1980s smash TV show *Magnum P.I.*, where the iconic title character made famous by Tom Selleck is now played by Jay Hernandez, who is of Mexican descent.

We want to note that these actors mentioned above didn't do something wrong by accepting these roles, even if they are in many ways problematic. The roles are what they are, and often the actors must make a difficult decision in choosing between what they would like to see and the realities of the roles available to them. Television and film media make up a business industry, and actors must often make a personal business decision.

Even with flashes of progress all around us, Latinxs continue to be cast in these small, stock, stereotypical roles even into the twenty-first century. No matter how many strides we make in the direction of progress, there will be the occurrence of something that reminds us how far we've yet to go. This is what makes things so frustrating for people invested in Latinx culture who are paying close attention to these developments. We get excited when we see Oscar Isaac as the lead in a Cohen Bros film like *Inside Llewyn Davis* (2013) or Poe Dameron in the newest *Star Wars Trilogy* or as Nathan, Ava's creator in the sci-fi thriller *Ex Machina* (2014). But then when we see Latinxs cast as a stereotype so fatigued that it can barely resist parody, we are annoyed and disappointed. Only more roles, unfettered from limited imaginations, will prove an elixir for this stubborn problem.

RESISTING THE BLOCKBUSTER'S HYPNOTIC POWERS

When Diego Luna's biopic *Cesar Chavez* (2014) opened the same weekend as Darren Aronofsky's *Noah* (as they actually did), Latinx audiences tended to shell out for the latter. Latinx filmgoers should be able to go and see any film. Yet we all know that films by Latinxs are

Cesar Chavez (played by Michael Peña) in *Cesar Chavez* (2016)

underviewed—and therefore undersupported. It's hard to resist the massive propaganda machinery that puts a *Noah* front and center over a *Cesar Chavez*.

Indeed, if *Cesar Chavez* had the same marketing power, it might have been as huge a hit as *Coco* was. We want our Latinx representation, but we also need the marketing machinery behind getting these hyped up enough to challenge and overcome those that feature, literally, white messiah figures—from *Noah* to *Avatar* and to nearly all of film history. It's about parity in representation *and* in getting the good Latinx word out.

A Reel and Real Wrap-Up

As we have begun to map out, the *reel* landscape that reconstructs *real* Latinxs is complex. Even when we do have Latinx portrayals, if they are marked as such, scholars and audiences will inevitably evaluate whether or not they're done well. And when we are represented as simply *there* in the *reel* world without readily identifiable markers of Latinidad, characters will be critiqued for being whitewashed. All of this is important, of course; otherwise we wouldn't be writing this book. However, it also reminds us that we have a long way to go.

CEOs and studio executives continue to gatekeep what's reconstructed in film and TV. That said, they exist in a capitalist society. To put it candidly, entertainment that makes money is given the opportunity. Perhaps with our critical pushes and boot slams as well as our pesos, they will get over their prejudices and wake to this fact.

Chapter 1

REEL MARKERS OF LATINIDAD

Real Demographics versus Reel Representation

The Latinx demographic numbers are more than abundant, yet we're still only a blip on the representational radar. To recall some statistics thrown out earlier, U.S. Latinxs are 18 percent of the population yet are less than 3 percent of those represented in all media. The ratios get worse when we start to consider specifics such as the percentage of main characters, speaking roles, and the like. We are at once *really* here and yet *reely* not here. We exist in a state of being present and yet absent in our presence. We are needed and yet not wanted.

Perhaps we should not be too surprised by this. Think about the labor history of U.S. Latinxs. The doors are open for Latinxs to work for minimum wage (in the best of cases) picking fruit and vegetables, washing dishes, cleaning toilets, or working grueling shifts at meat processing plants. The doors are essentially closed to us for education access that can lead to our becoming writers or filmmakers for TV or film—or professors like us. The National Center for Education Statistics puts some percentages to what we already know and experience firsthand. The professoriate is largely made up of white men (42 percent) and women (35 percent), with Latinxs (men and women) coming in at only 2 percent (right behind African Americans at 3 percent). The racial demographics that make up mainstream film and TV media production are even more lopsided.

While Latinx reel presence has grown since the 1960s and 1970s, so, too, have our demographic numbers. So while today we're less likely to appear as gardeners, mechanics, or maids (and this thanks to the door pounding of actors like Cesar Romero and Anthony Quinn), we're still disproportionally absent. Latinxs continue to live in this paradoxical space of having value and worth while simultaneously *not being seen* as of value or importance.

Let's just call it for what it is. Within the mainstream film and TV landscape, white characters don't need markers to be seen as the norm or default. They have narrative plentitude, as Nguyen reminds us. When it comes to representing Latinidad, the ethnoracial mainstream media schemas *mark* ethnicity in exaggerated yet deliberate ways. When not whitewashing, mainstream media likes to go for easily identifiable, ethnoracially marked bodies. Latinxs swing on an ethnoracial pendulum between exaggerated presence (Ugly Betty's poncho or Sofía Vergara's hyperexaggerated accent, for instance) to absence (Demi Lovato's typical roles for Disney). We also see this same absent-presence impulse in the casting of racially marked bodies

Armando Muñoz "Darwin" (played by Edi Gathegi) in *X-Men: First Class* (2011)

(usually African Americans) to play Latinx characters in the comic-book film universe. For instance, in *X-Men: First Class*, Brian Vaughn cast Kenyan-born actor Edi Gathegi to play the original comic-book Latinx mutant character Armando Muñoz ("Darwin").

Latinxs can and do look like all races or ethnicities. Studio executives don't understand what Latinxs can look like, or rather, the *possibilities* of what they *can* look like. Mainstream media and audiences struggle with this fact. Thus, when we have the fair-skinned, blond-haired, and blue-eyed Latina Cameron Diaz on screen, the tendency is to allow her to "pass" and give her no ethnic markers whatsoever. In a majority of her films, she does not have a Hispanic name, she speaks no Spanish, has no discernible accent, doesn't eat menudo for dinner, and so on. In her case, to give her ethnic markers on the screen might serve only to confuse audiences. A similar issue may be the case with other Hispanic groups that are often aligned with Latinxs, such as Martin Sheen and his sons Emilio Estevez and Charlie Sheen. They are of Hispanic heritage (Spanish Irish, specifically), but that heritage is never marked or identified on the screen.

Here we ask whether it's the writers, directors, executive producers, or the actors who are the ones responsible for creating a *reel* imaginary filled with passing-as-white Latinxs. In the case of Demi Lovato, Selena Gomez, and Cristina Aguilera, their ethnicity is rarely used as a strong feature of their characterization in Disney media. But it's not exactly erased, as it is in the case of Cameron Diaz or the Sheens. We think of Disney's *Stuck in the Middle* or *Wizards of Waverly Place*, which feature Latinx families (in the case of *Wizards* a mixed Italian Latinx family) with just enough ethnoracial sprinkles to give them a light dusting of Latinidad. These are not the families we saw in *The George Lopez Show* or in the more recent all-Latinx *familia* reboot of *One Day at a Time*. There we have ethnoracial markings but in a smart way. The writing, characters, and story lines *know* the stereotypes and turn them upside down. Another way to think about this would be that whereas *Stuck in the Middle* and others are created for non-Latinx ideal audiences, shows such as *George Lopez* and *One Day* clearly have front and center complexly layered Latinx audiences.

Deep Histories of Ethnoracial Media Markings

Film and TV's pendulum swing between an exaggerated presence and total absence of Latinxs has a long history. Whether it is packs of violent sociopaths when they attack (rape?) Susie (Janet Leigh) in *Touch of Evil* (1958) or Lupe Véles (née María Guadalupe Vélez de Villalobos) in *Mexican Spitfire* (1940) or Rita Hayworth (née Margarita Carmen Cansino and known as "Rita the Cheetah") in *Untamed* (1955), egregious caricatures became the unfortunate bedrock of Latinx representation in Hollywood. Silver-screen reconstructions of Latinas as "spitfires"—Raquel Welch, Dolores del Río, Rita Moreno (*West Side Story*), and many others—constrained Latinas in terms of the roles they could play. The same holds for bandito figures and brown-skinned criminals as ready-made villains. Hollywood has a long, deep history of presenting Latinx ethnoraciality as transgressive, violent, hypersexual, uncivil, and unlawful, and this history has been difficult to rectify.

The reconstruction of these Latinas as consumable "spitfires" created the Latina bombshell stereotype in Hollywood. These women, like many in Hollywood, even white women, had to undergo

Carmelita Fuentes (played by Lupe Vélez) in *Mexican Spitfire* (1940)

significant transformations. Norma Jean Mortenson was compelled to become an icon of beauty and sexuality in the United States, only we know her by her more famous name, Marilyn Monroe. Her well-documented rise and fall are closely linked to the pressures of conforming to Hollywood's vision for her. Hayworth and Véles underwent similar pressures with the added stress of the erasing of their heritage.

And the pendulum has swung in the opposite direction, unmarking us ethnoracially. How many people knew that Anthony Quinn (né

Antonio Rodolfo Quinn) was born in Mexico and grew up in Latinx borderland spaces such as El Paso and Boyle Heights? For a paycheck, Quinn became adept at playing ethnoracially ambiguous *and* exaggerated roles: from ethnically ambiguous swashbuckling villains to Zorba the Greek. He was continuously cast in the role of the Other, from Indians and Mafia dons to Chinese guerrillas and Arab bandits.

It's not necessarily that he didn't want the Latinx roles. He did. Famously, he wanted the role of Emiliano Zapata in Kazan's *Viva Zapata!* (1952), but Steinbeck (screenplay author) insisted it go to Brando. (Notably, Steinbeck also made Zapata illiterate and requested that Zapata's love interest, "Soldadera"—played by the Mexican-born actress known as "Margo"—be depicted as a rural woman-girl "with a kind of savage

animal beauty.") Quinn got to play the brother, Eufemio. Brando was one of the top stars in Hollywood at the time, and Steinbeck certainly wanted Brando as the star not because he thought it would be more authentic or true to the spirit of Zapata's character (that's laughable) but because he wanted the film based on his screenplay to be a box-office success.

Eufemio Zapata (played by Anthony Quinn) in *Viva Zapata!* (1952)

Steinbeck and Kazan in this instance are emblematic of much of Hollywood film production. Studios that aim for a great number of ticket sales realize they are not making factual, historically accurate documentaries. It is a rare occurrence when these executives go to the trouble of ensuring accuracy and authenticity. We know this is a defining attribute of the film and TV industry, which is why we get egregious castings that make us wonder what they were thinking.

In the end, Quinn's transmutability on the screen ultimately proved to be a material asset. He had a long Hollywood career and a lifetime of steady income and fame. He was the first Latinx to win an Academy Award for supporting actor. And his accomplishments as a Latinx in Hollywood seem to be recognized after the fact. Imprints of his hands and feet are there on the sidewalk outside Grauman's Chinese Theatre, and in Chihuahua, Mexico, there is a statue of him doing his "Zorba the Greek" dance.

Along these same lines, there are some Latinx actors who did not (could not?) transmute their identity on the screen. In the 1980s and 1990s, María Conchita Alonzo's mestizo looks, brown skin, dark hair, and her significant Spanish-accented English were traits that, combined, disallowed her from playing anything other than a Latina.

Rare is the dark and mestizo-looking (indigenous and/or African featured) Latinx actor who is cast in a role that bears no characteristics of Latinidad. We have less than a handful: Edward James Olmos as Gaff in Ridley Scott's *Blade Runner*. His first name is Eduardo, but we never actually hear this in the film. The only marker of his Latinidad is *Olmos himself*. We see the same with gay blatinx actor Wilson Cruz cast as Dr. Culber (a French-sounding last name) in CBS's *Star Trek: Discovery* (2017–). The only marker of his Afro-Latinidad is *himself*.

We see the same erasure of a complex mestizo ancestry when TV and film exaggeratedly *indigenize* Latinx actors. Self-identified Latindio (Mexican and Native) Robert Beltran was cast as Commander Chakotay in the TV series *Star Trek: Voyager*. While he carved out a significant role for a Latinx actor and with this cleared space in the Star Trek universe for people of color, his character (the last name and speech intonations and patterns) was more Native than Latinx.

We continue to have egregious, risible representations of minority communities nearly twenty years into the twenty-first century. When *Viva Zapata!* was released in 1952, people thought that today we would be using flying cars, eating food in pill form, and watching a sunrise on the planet Mars. How have these terrible representations continued to be perpetuated nearly seventy years after *Viva Zapata!* in 1952? Over twice as many years have passed since *Zapata!* than the interval between that film and the actual assassination of Emiliano Zapata himself. Yet the stereotypical representations of Latinxs continue and with great plenitude.

Latinxs and the Social-Realist Narrative

Ironically, Anthony Quinn, whose career was determined by a racist Hollywood, also went on to play the character Sanchez in the film re-creation of Oscar Lewis's controversial *Children of Sanchez* (1961). Lewis's formulation of a cycle of poverty makes huge deterministic claims about us Latinxs based on a study of one Mexican family. It is true that a lack of social mobility has been endemic in Mexico, where half the population is poor. We Latinxs often appear in social-realist narratives. Why is that? Because it is a position that makes many non-Latinxs feel some sympathy for Latinxs. America loves a "pull yourself up by your bootstraps" story, the kind of story that dominated the early twentieth-century American literary landscape.

Influential editor William Dean Howells figuratively came to embody this type of storytelling. But we know that success and failure, even in the United States, are not simply a matter of individual effort despite the myths of the American dream we have been told. One has to take a quick look at stories featuring Latinxs in the United States, and many written by Latinxs, that take on the story of the impoverished Latinx family who has to survive and, potentially, triumph in some way—what Christopher González has called the "barrio bildungsroman." Quinn's turn as Sanchez, though ironic, is but one example of how Hollywood has historically portrayed Latinxs in their stories. Though many in Mexico, and Latinxs in the United States for that matter, find themselves not as socially mobile as they would like, many are in positions with mobility thanks to serendipity, hard work, and education.

Reel Latinxs in Time and Place

Anthony Quinn made his mark in Hollywood by crafting timeless performances on screen, and he was rewarded with the highest award he could receive—the Oscar. After having scaled the summit of Olympus, he could embrace his Latinx heritage more fully. Indeed, as the twentieth century waned, there was an unquestioned awareness of and exposure to Latinx culture in the United States. That Quinn began to be more engaged with his Latinx heritage is not as surprising as it might seem at first. He was a terrific and legendary actor, and the Latinx community is right to embrace his legacy to the fullest. He remains an example of what Latinxs can do if given the chance even if the system in which he found himself compelled him to make many rather difficult choices concerning his heritage and ancestry. This form of passing in Hollywood was a naturalized process, and many ethnic actors had to inhabit an identity that was more aligned with white American culture.

In the early days of Hollywood's distillation and reconstruction of real Latinx subjects, there was this consistent pattern to whitewash (change her name or pluck her eyebrows, as with Hayworth) *and* to exaggerate the sexually transgressive. This was also true with Latinx men. For example, Mexican-born Ramón Novarro (né Jose Ramón Gil Samaniego) stripped down his name to make it more palatable for a U.S. movie consumer. Second cousin to Dolores del Río (née María de los Dolores Asúnsolo López-Negrete), Ramón Novarro—MGM's marquee Latin lover—made upward of $100,000 a film. And, as it turns out, he was passing with his performances as a straight Latin lover when in fact Novarro was gay. Like his queer white compadres, such as Rock Hudson, there's no way one could be *out* during most of the twentieth century in Hollywood. Even after Hudson was outed (the media got wind of his being HIV positive and that his death was due to AIDS), many straight audiences didn't want to believe he was gay. That Novarro was Latinx *and* gay added a further layer. Tragically, this led to his ultimate annihilation—not just through drugs and alcohol, but also in his murder by two gay prostitutes in 1968.

Charles Bukowski fictionalized Novarro's murder in his violent and brutal short story, "The Murder of Ramon Vasquez," which appeared in his *Erections, Ejaculations and General Tales of Ordinary Madness* (1972). Yet again, we return to that "slumming" tradition we mentioned earlier in the book. The tragic lives of Latinxs make excellent fodder for the fictions of white writers. Whether Bukowski, Kerouac, Burroughs, or many, many others, there's a long tradition of slumming it in Latinx lives, with the more tragic making for the more enticing stories. It reminds one of the commodification of Latinxs—their bodies, their looks, their lives, their legacies.

Latinxs after the Talkies

Dolores del Río rose to fame pretalkies. Then, with the introduction of sound, audiences could potentially hear her accent—an arguably uncontrollable marker of her Latinidad. When a Latinx actor crosses the line of being "too Latinx," it becomes a distraction and makes Hollywood hesitate. There appears to be a tipping point when it comes to how far Hollywood executives will bend in terms of allowing ethnoracial representation on the silver screen before they snap and say no more. Now, time has shown that Hollywood has increased its flexibility, but it is still liable to only go so far on a consistent basis. We still relish those moments, however, when we are witness to extraordinary breakthroughs in Latinx representation on the screen.

One way or another, the arrival of voice reproduction with the talkies seemed to racialize these Latinx stars. It ended the careers of the Latin lovers such as Novarro and Moreno, but it also seemed to ring the death knoll to del Río's career—at least in the United States. After the witch hunt in 1934—where she was accused of promoting communism in California because of her affiliation with Diego Rivera, Frida Kahlo, Charles Chaplin, and Orson Welles—she moved back to Mexico, where her looks and accent didn't scare audiences with a so-called exotic persona. Here she had a second career as a film star.

Latinxs had to fit a certain *look*, and they also had to sound "white." Other sorts of accents were deemed acceptable—consider Received Pronunciation and the mid-Atlantic accent that Hollywood took such pains to propagate. This became entrenched in the minds and expectations of moviegoing audiences.

Yet there was also that swing of the pendulum to the exaggerated *sound* presence. Think of Latinxs like Ricardo Montalbán in cinema and Desi Arnaz on TV in the 1950s. Both of these men in particular had very pronounced Spanish accents, and Arnaz even incorporated a running gag where Lucy, and notably only Lucy, teased him about his accent. In time the Latinx actor with the pronounced accent became a part of the Latin-lover mystique once more. Think, too, of Julio Iglesias in the music world and his son, Enrique, who both fit this mold in the American consciousness. And later there was the advent of Antonio Banderas. Even Latinas in cinema ultimately were "allowed" to have Spanish accents—Salma Hayek, Penélope Cruz, and Sofía Vergara, to name but three.

Latinxs and Early Westerns

There's been a long tradition of Latinx actors appearing in Westerns as Latinxs. Antonio Moreno played Emilio Figueroa in *The Searchers*

(1955), considered to be one of John Ford's masterpieces. However, the Latinx characters were either banditos or hapless campesinos inhabiting the shadows thrown by Indian-murdering white saviors such as John Wayne. In real life, John Wayne was married three times, all to Latinas. But on screen both Wayne and John Ford made sure that American filmgoing audiences knew how the West was won, that is, by good white men who braved hostile savages with dark complexions. From D. W. Griffith's *Birth of a Nation* to the huge popularity of the Western flicks in the fifties, the roots of American cinema were founded on white supremacy.

Hollywood cannot get away from the white-savior myth. At the moment, we are talking about the early decades of cinema, but the white savior has persisted well into the twenty-first century. It also has us scratching our heads. In many of our lives we've had a white savior—a school teacher or role model who recognized our potential and helped open doors. There's the anecdote James Baldwin relates in "Notes of a Native Son" where he describes his white teacher who saw something special in young James and sought to take him on enrichment activities—undertakings James knew his father would never allow. In a sense, he tricked his father by having the white teacher come to his home without letting his parents know she was white. Once she was there, her whiteness would preclude James's father from refusing.

Here, again, we have another instance of the difficulties minority communities encounter. While the white savior is a pernicious and stubborn story, we see over and over again in history that there have been, for lack of a better term, white saviors. It's why films like *Dances with Wolves* (1990), *The Blind Side* (2009), *Avatar*, and *McFarlane, USA* (2015), continue to be made—all are told from the perspective of the white-savior character as protagonist rather than the character of color who does much of the hard work to rise above his or her circumstances.

From Latinx Lover to Greaser Gangbanger

As much as the Latin lover was a phenomenon, so too was the greaser figure. And if we turn film history back to some of its origin stories, we ask, what's more offensive, *Birth of a Nation* or Griffith's *The Greaser's Gauntlet* (1908), with Wilfred Lucas in brownface as José. At that time, greaser did not mean greased style of hair as it does with Travolta slicking back his hair in *Grease*. In the early part of the century, and before that in the nineteenth century with the passage of California's Greaser Act of 1855, *greaser* was a racist term used to denigrate Mexicans. Rather than identify those who earned a living greasing wagon axles and animal hides, its connotations of slime and dirtiness became denotative derogatory stand-ins for all Mexicans.

Griffith's *Birth of a Nation* offends deeply because it positions itself as a kind of founding document for the idea of the United States as a white supremacist's utopia in the making. It portrays whites as saviors sent from on high to tame a savage nation, but it is mythological in its reach. That is not to say *The Greaser's Gauntlet* is not terrible in its representation of Latinxs. But rather than excoriate Griffith, which he well deserves, let's think of these films as Exhibit A of Hollywood's racist roots. They are so deeply entrenched that they trace back to some of the industry's founding films. Therein lies the current value of Griffith and his lamentable films—they reveal just how deeply ingrained racism and white-supremacist ideology were in the industry. Not only was it in the "birth of a nation"; racism permeated the "birth of an industry."

The Curious History of Brownface

We mentioned earlier that while Quinn wanted the role of Zapata, Marlon Brando got it, and Alan Reed got the role of Pancho Villa. Even before this, Europeans were cast to play Latinx characters: Austro-Hungarian American Jewish actor Paul Muni played Johnnie Ramirez in Archie Mayo's social-realist drama *Bordertown* (1935). And Charlton Heston played Mexican ambassador Miguel "Mike" Vargas in Orson Welles's *Touch of Evil* (1958). Some have let the Hollywood of this epoch off the hook, arguing either for the star power of the white actor playing the Latinx character or identifying this as a period when black- and brownface were completely unproblematic.

Yet we still confront the issue of black- and brownface today. It's still happening. There's the casting of Spaniards such as Penélope Cruz, Paz Vega, and Antonio Banderas as Latinxs.

Our culture, our heritage is desirable as a kind of Othered, exotic commodity. Hollywood cinema wants to represent an idea or an

Johnnie Ramirez (played by Paul Muni) in *Bordertown* (1935)

essentialist notion of who Latinxs are, but they want to do it without Latinx participation. That alone says much about whiteness in Hollywood and about how the most base and lazy stereotypes persist.

Stereotypes

A quick excursus about stereotypes, which have been discussed and parsed to great degree in other venues, bears mentioning here. Stereotypes, as a construct, are not evil or harmful as a storytelling *device*. Sometimes in storytelling—filmic or otherwise—the storyteller doesn't have the time or space for full and nuanced characterization. Sometimes a narrative needs a panhandler on the street to beg for change in order to drive the plot along, or maybe it's a nameless doctor telling the protagonist that she has two weeks to live. There, stereotypes fulfill a narrative function. Yet an identity group must be allowed to be more than the sum total of a stereotype. If Latinxs are only ever prison inmates or drug dealers or spousal abusers, then that does harm to any complex conception of what it means to be Latinx in the United States.

Similarly, we can denounce brownface once and for all. At the time of the examples mentioned, few Latinxs were given substantive roles in Hollywood films; therefore, we see brownface. That speaks to the hubris of white privilege and white supremacy. Who can act like a Latinx on screen without casting a Latinx? Why, a white actor, of course! In fact, the white actor is most likely a better actor anyway . . . and isn't this about "acting"? Why can't a white actor be cast as a Latinx? Such is the rationalization of this unfortunate practice even in recent years. Now, rather than pretend white actors are characters from melanin-infused cultures, studios simply cast white actors in the roles of ancient Egyptians or from other non-Anglo cultures. We look back to the mid-twentieth century and see Charlton Heston as Moses and

Laurence Olivier as Othello, John Wayne as Ghengis Khan in *The Conqueror* (1956), Natalie Wood as Maria in *West Side Story* (1961)—and even more recently Jim Caviezel as Jesus of Nazareth in *The Passion of the Christ* and Russell Crowe as the lead in *Noah*. Or take the film *Gods of Egypt* and recognize how it's not even about brownface, it's about boldface erasure.

The other phenomenon at play here is the browning of Spaniards as Latinxs. This happens in part because a good portion of the U.S. non-Latinx moviegoing audience doesn't really know the difference between a Spaniard, a Latin American, or a US Latinx. It's a confusion and conflation that happens to Latinxs every day

María Álvarez (played by Penélope Cruz) in *Bandidas* (2006)

when non-Latinxs refer to us as "Spanish." It should come as little surprise that a Banderas, a Cruz, or a Sofía Vergara are cast as U.S. Latinxs.

Now is a good time to emphasize the difference between an immigrant to the United States who hails from a Latin American nation and a person of Latinx heritage who is born in the United States. The experiences and identities of these individuals do not neatly align, and yet the greater mainstream society seeks to categorize *all* Spanish-speaking peoples, or peoples with a Spanish-speaking ancestor from a Latin American country, as the same. Such a process of homogenization is used for political strength, but opponents of such a process rightly note that it flattens out all Latinidad as having just a few shared characteristics.

Film and TV creators continue to show a preference for all things European. The real question is, Should a Spaniard take the role of a Mexican? Should a Mexican play the part of a Honduran?

Mainstream Preferences for Euro-Featured Latinxs

Most Latinx movie stars do not have so-called *indio* features. From those who crossed the border—such as Salma Hayek, Ana de la

Reguera, Demián Bichir, Gael García Bernal, and Diego Luna—to those Latinxs this side of the border—for example, Cameron Diaz and Andy García (né Andrés Arturo García Menéndez)—there's a preference, an obsession, with whiteness, with the light-skinned Latinx. For many decades, the only *indio*-looking Latinxs we saw were simple stereotypes (and even then, why bother hiring a Latinx when we can just put a white extra in brownface?), or they appeared in self-produced, self-made films by Latinxs.

Let's consider Cameron Michelle Diaz for a minute. As far as the world was concerned, she wasn't Latina—at least until the release of *Bad Teacher* (2011). In that film she played a character who was, well, bad. She was immoral, a gold-digging middle school teacher who cursed at her students, drank heavily, and smoked pot. It seemed a

safe moment to invest fully in her *bad* identity, letting people know in interviews all over the media that she was Latina: born in San Diego to a family of Cuban cigar rollers from Tampa's Ybor City. We ask, Why not mention her Latinidad while promoting her breakout 1994 film with Jim Carrey, *The Mask*, or her smash 1998 hit, *There's Something about Mary*? We don't know for certain why, but we can see that her Latina heritage was discussed much more when she played the role of an oversexed, rule-

Elizabeth Halsey (played by Cameron Diaz) in *Bad Teacher* (2011)

breaking educator in *Bad Teacher*. This is a reminder that deviant Latinxs are perhaps more interesting in Hollywood than otherwise.

The first time Cameron Diaz was cast as a Latina was in Ridley Scott's *The Counselor* (2013)—along with Euro-Spaniards Javier Bardem and Penélope Cruz, also cast as Latinxs. We could call this out as another example of Hollywood's obsession with whiteness/Europeanness. We can also see it as an exemplar exception to the brown mestizo conception that many Americans have of Latinxs. But we know that if you travel to Latin America, you will see a multitude of Latin Americans who fit the Cameron Diaz mold—fair skinned, blue eyed, blond haired. Just turn on a telenovela and wait a few minutes. But in the United States, Diaz is an extreme exception to the rule that dominates how Latinas are cast and how they are represented on the screen. Perhaps, however, we can really celebrate this potentiality when she chooses to play characters clearly identified as Latinas, discusses her own Latina heritage, and aligns herself with issues that affect Latinxs in the United States.

During the 1990s, a series of animated shorts appeared occasionally on *Saturday Night Live* called "The Ambiguously Gay Duo." It featured a superhero duo in the mold of Batman and Robin and a running gag that everything the duo seemed to do revealed an obvious innuendo concerning their gayness. Because of the diversity in our looks, ancestry, and linguistic register, Latinxs are cast as ambiguously ethnic. We can sometimes play an Italian or a Middle Eastern character, or sometimes a Greek or Native American. Isn't this a bit beyond the pale? Beyond laughable? It's acting *and* representation that matter. There are real-world implications from such casting decisions. Latinxs benefit from this sliding ethnicity on the screen, and yet they have historically been erased by actors of other ethnicities in much the same way.

Latinx Mestizos Here and Elsewhere

There are important exceptions. We think readily of Jimmy Smits, Lou Diamond Phillips, and Salma Hayek. While Phillips is Filipino Scottish Irish, he's more mestizo looking than, say, Ricky Martin. Consider Hayek's darker complexion, dark hair, and body shape. Her breakthrough in Hollywood and her subsequent experiences—which she revealed in a devastating op-ed in the *New York Times* during the Harvey Weinstein revelations and the #MeToo movement—really helped change conceptions of the more mestiza-looking Latina in Hollywood.

Let's not forget, too, that it was Luis Valdez who cast Lou Diamond Phillips and Esai Morales as Latinx characters in touch with their mestizo ancestry in *La Bamba*. We see this in Robert Rodriguez's casting as well. He, too, has cast many actors with *darker Latinx* features in his films: Danny Trejo, Michelle Rodriguez, and Hayek,

Static tableaux representation of mestizaje
¡Que viva México! (1930)

among others. That is, these more *ethnic-looking* Latinxs tend to appear in films outside the Hollywood system.

The impulse to romanticize the mestizo never stuck here like it did south of the border in Mexico. In Mexico, we don't have that same legacy of sentimental portrayals that abstract the mestizo from reality (frozen in some nostalgic past), as seen in Sergei Eisenstein's *¡Que Viva Mexico!* (1931) and later continued in the Mexican Golden Age with Eisenstein's disciple, Gabriel Figueroa—and, of course, El Indio Fernández.

Part of this is because Mexico doesn't share this same ideology of manifest destiny—the taming of the West as a contest between white pioneers and brown savages. In this formulation, Native Americans and Mexicans in the United States were conflated as the same sort of brute who could easily be defeated by the sophistication and intelligence of the white cowboy or soldier. Native Americans, unlike Latinxs, were cast as the noble savage in American storytelling as early as the Leatherstocking tales by James Fenimore Cooper—a tragic figure, akin to the idea of the Romanticization of the mestizo in Mexico, conceived of as essentially a good person but a necessary sacrifice for the progress and development of the United States.

The mestizo, the hybrid of the indigenous and the European colonizer, has rarely enjoyed the same sort of tragic status as the noble savage. That is, not if white storytellers with access to filmmaking and storytelling are in control. Latinxs have worked hard to reclaim this sense of respect for mestizos in their own storytelling.

Latinx Passing

Let's just state at the outset that Latinx passing does not operate the same as it does in the African American community. There are similarities, however. Skin tone is an undeniably important aspect of passing. The lighter a person's skin tone, the greater chance that person may pass. Similarly, linguistic facility in so-called standard English is also of significance. African Americans and Latinxs can easily be accused of "sounding white" by using standard English, and it is a form of passing as well.

On a personal note, we both recognize that Christopher's skin is naturally darker than Frederick's. However, people often look past Christopher's skin color and phenotype because of the way he speaks, which is without accent, articulate, and educated. Yet this same manner of speaking for both Frederick and Christopher has generated insults from childhood friends and cousins: we sound white and are even accused of trying to *be white*. So Latinxs may sometimes have the option to pass, but it is not without consequence, both positive and negative.

Martin Sheen was born Ramón Gerard Antonio Estévez to an Irish American mother and Spanish father (from Galicia, Spain). Robert Rodriguez turns this all upside down and inside out in *Machete Kills* (2013). Rodriguez chooses to announce in the credits Charlie Sheen with his actual birth name, Carlos Estevez. Yet Martin's younger son, Emilio, kept the family's last name, Estevez. He has had a seemingly successful career. He made his break (and was later identified with those who made up the eighties-era Brat Pack) playing the drunken "greaser" character Two-Bit Matthews in *The Outsiders* (1982). He played the jock archetype in John Hughes's classic *The Breakfast Club* with no hint in the film that he is Hispanic. In fact, we see the character's father at the film's opening, clearly coded as a white man. Estevez rarely played a Latinx because he had all the elements of passing—fair skinned, golden hair, light eyes—except the name. Does this mean that you can keep a Hispanic name if you "look" white? We might ask the same of Martin Sheen and Charlie Sheen, though Martin is of the generation that would be compelled to change his name.

Let's not forget Cameron Diaz. She didn't change a thing about herself, but it seemed audiences and the media did the passing for her—as if they ignored the fact that her surname is Diaz and she is of Latinx heritage. This is yet another kind of invisibility—an invisibility where the audience is willingly blindfolded.

Whether it's an actor or it's the systemic media structures, when Latinxs pass there are material and psychic consequences. There is always a cost of doing the business of passing, and it must affect a person's sense of self and identity when it happens. It is worse for the individual when he or she is compelled to pass. There are instances where a complete change must occur—hair color, eye color, skin lightening, erasure of an accent, the changing of a name, etc. Such a person is literally becoming another person—not just in a role, but in an identity.

Passing in Reel Stories

In the televisual imaginary, passing and upward mobility go hand in hand. Recall that Betty (America Ferrera) turns from poor and thus "ugly" (she has "bad taste" in clothes) to successful upper middle class and thus beautiful (she has good taste in clothes and men, including especially her paleface boss).

The show increasingly subordinates the presence of her Latinidad as she moves up the ladder to the point where she leaves the space of

Mexican food, sounds, movements, and linguistic code-switching for London. The show ends with Betty leaving behind her unemployed single-mother sister, Hilda (Ana Ortiz); her gay nephew, Justin Suarez (played by Italian Puerto Rican actor Mark Indelicato); and father, Ignacio (played by Cuban American actor Tony Plana).

Betty Suarez (played by America Ferrera) in *Ugly Betty* (season 1, episode 1, 2006)

Cinderella stories of Latinx passing, like *Ugly Betty* and *Maid in Manhattan* and so many others, are omnipresent. We shouldn't be surprised by this. Because white ideology and history are dominant discourses in the United States, it seems logical that Latinxs would have to imbibe in such whiteness in order to continue to move up the social ladder.

Betty Suarez (played by America Ferrera) with Daniel Meade (played by Eric Mabius) in *Ugly Betty* (season 4, episode 20, 2010)

That is unsurprising to be sure, and it seems to reflect a tangible, material reality that Latinxs face all the time. Our last comment is a tough pill to swallow. In order to attain success, Latinxs often have to leave home and the ones they love so that they may realize their full potential. But Latinxs tend to be very family oriented, and the expectation is that one stays close to home. So when Betty wants to leave and experience something new, we don't fault her. What we fault is what's dangling at the end of the rope: the straight, white romance and patriarchal system that undergird her life choices.

We pass geographic lines, too. Time and time again in TV and films, we're seen crossing from somewhere south of the U.S.-Mexico border. The scriptwriters of *Modern Family* constantly remind us of this in the writing of Gloria's character. We see the same with the writing of the *mamá* character in *Cristela*. And the heavy use of the telenovela conceit in shaping the TV show *Jane the Virgin* (a U.S. re-creation of the Venezuelan telenovela *Juana la virgen*) does the same. We see it in Latinx-made films as well. Think of Nava's *El Norte* (1983), Patricia Riggen's more recent *La misma luna* (2007), and Demian Bichir as undocumented *jardinero* Carlos Galindo, in Chris Weitz's *A Better Life* (2011).

We've crossed the border—and we can never rid ourselves of it. It becomes a part of our psychic baggage.

In many ways, the border defines Latinxs for a majority of American audiences. Although it is true that many Latinxs have had to

Carlos Galindo (*right*, played by Demián Bichir) in *A Better Life* (2011)

contend with a border in some way or another, there are literally *millions* of Latinxs in the United States who have never crossed the border except to take a vacation. The border-crossing narrative is often portrayed as a dramatic event, and it is always politically timely, so it plays well as a story line. Certainly we also want new and fresh ideas for how Latinxs appear in our films and on TV, but the border-crossing trope is a profitable one for many studios, and so they will continue to go to the well, or in this case the border, until border stories are no longer of interest. Or, more accurately, profitable.

Passing happens, too, with the choice of location. Director John McTiernan filmed in Mexico to create a fictional Latin America in *Predator* (1987). Sergio Leone shot all his story worlds' U.S.-Mexico borderlands outside of Madrid, Spain. More contemporary directors tend to choose Latinx settings to urbanize and make more dangerous their film stories—and this no matter the race of the director. In making *2 Fast 2 Furious* (2003), African American director John Singleton chose as his backdrops Miami and California, emphasizing the tempestuous, dangerous Latinidad of Eva Mendes as Monica Fuentes. Not only are Latinxs as a people and as a culture stereotyped, geographic areas Latinxs call home tend to embody the worst of the culture. Nothing is going to happen in a middle-class suburb, so create a story about murderous cartels in the U.S.-Mexico borderlands, as with the recent *Sicario* (2015) and *Sicario 2: Day of Soldado* (2018).

We see this even more exaggeratedly in Neil Blomkamp's *Elysium* (2013), which puts center stage issues of poverty for the majority and

Latinxs in a postapocalyptic Los Angeles in *Elysium* (2013)

eternal life for the 1 percent (living in a space habitat aptly named Elysium, which "illegal" ships launch from Earth to try to reach) but does so by identifying that poverty as Latinx made and inhabited—a set that makes the Anglo savior Max Da Costa (Matt Damon, after Eminem turned it down) shine out even more. *Elysium* has it all— white savior, wretchedness of the border, criminality among Latinxs.

It would have been much more daring to cast a Latinx in the protagonist role, but having Matt Damon as the lead and suddenly to have his situation take a drastic turn for the worst undermines his white privilege and allows him to align himself with the Latinxs in his sphere. He was adopted by a Latinx family, and he sees himself in both Latinx and white spheres of experience. Not as good a film as Blomkamp's *District 9*, but it has the same impetus—a privileged character suddenly becomes one of the disenfranchised.

Resistant Latinx Reels

Let's not forget, though, that there are films that push against the white-savior, passing, brownface schemas that make up the bulk of the film and TV imaginary. For instance, *Napoleon Dynamite* has fun with Latinx culture, and it's set in southern Idaho near Utah—a place not necessarily known for its Latinxs (at least in film, anyway). And there's Puerto Rican Miguel Arteta's *Star Maps* (1997) and his *Beatriz at Dinner* (2017). Arturo Aldama discusses the film as resistant border cinematic text (it throws punches or *chingazos* of subaltern resistance) that reconstructs how the mainstream commodifies *los recíen llegado* and Latinxs generally. For Aldama, the film calls attention to how Latinx families have also internalized pathological gender-power relations. Indeed, the first generation (the *recién llegado*) is in such an interstitial space, and it is a position that is easily exploitable. To that end, it is a good position in which to showcase resistance and an awareness that the ideological powers and institutions of both nations ever seek to exploit these peoples in some fashion or form. We can think of *Beatriz at Dinner* as also a border story. Beatriz (Salma Hayek) traverses borders of class and race, forcing centers of white privilege to face their own restrictive class and race-based ideologies. And there are those stories that physically cross borders, such Cary Joji Fukunaga's *Sin nombre* (2009). The film literally ends just as the border is crossed.

Reel Latinxs as Good Subjects

We do appear as "good" subjects, but in stereotypical ways. For Latinxs, we become "good" through some redemptive means. This could be turning from gangbanging to the classroom in films like *Stand and Deliver*, or the tug of a child that turns us from our angry, destructive ways, as in a film like *My Family*. But we ask, are redemption narratives almost always applicable to Latinxs depicted as the down-and-out who rise to the top? Does this really reflect reality, or is that the reality mainstream America has conceived for Latinxs?

It is a stereotypical pattern, and yet many Latinx filmmakers, such as Edward James Olmos, are behind some of these films, such as his *American Me*. So the argument goes that a filmmaker and actor like Olmos, who has some say in the films he helms, should avoid stereotypical representations of Latinxs because he should know better. On the other hand, though these films are in those tried-and-true areas of Latinx culture, they're not bad films. The problem is that when there is a dearth of films that emphasize Latinx culture, then these sorts of films seem to carry greater stereotypical cachet. In effect, they overrepresent because there are not more films to consider. When audiences see white actors as white characters involved in crime, drug dealing, prostitution, and prison, they are not then convinced that all whites are these sorts of criminals precisely because audiences see whites in a myriad of roles. If Latinxs appeared in hundreds and thousands of films per year in all manner of roles, then we wouldn't be talking about this issue.

Reel Virgins and Whores

While Latinas move up (and sometimes down) the socioeconomic ladder and with this recoded as good or bad, more often they are presented as fated to be good (virgin) or bad (whore). Think of the way Jennifer Lopez appears in her music videos of late compared with her film roles. For instance, as Marisa Ava Marie Ventura in *Maid in Manhattan* (2002), she's a doe-eyed Latina who swoons to the eye of British Christopher Marshall (Ralph Fiennes).

Marisa Ventura (played by Jennifer Lopez) in *Maid in Manhattan* (2002)

The moral of the story is not that those around her accuse her of being bad (they think she stole a fur coat) but that if one is a good Latina, the white wealthy gentleman will forgive and then marry you, and all your socioeconomic problems will be solved. To put it simply, Latinas are portrayed as either sinners or saints. However, we see this also in our Latinx history, religion, and mythology: La Malinche, La Llorona, La Virgen de Guadalupe, and others. This is where patriarchy cuts across ethnoracial divides.

Good things come to the good Latina. We see this also in James L. Brooks's *Spanglish* (2004), where the Latina working maid and single mom Flor Moreno (played by Spaniard Paz Vega) has an opportunity to lasso the wealthy Anglo boss John Clasky (Adam Sandler), but she chooses not to break up this already dysfunctional family. She speaks in broken English, asking her daughter, "Is what you want for yourself to become someone very different than me?" She chooses virtue over vice and is rewarded in spades: her daughter Cristina (Shelbie Bruce) grows up with the possibility of going to Princeton University. The idea of the virtuous and chaste Latina pervades these narratives. They have to play nice and be good in opposition to the bad Latina spitfire, who is free spirited and untamed but must ultimately be "tamed" by the end of story. Here we have patriarchy at work again.

Bad to Good: Reel Snakes and Ladders

We pass as "good" citizens—that is, as upper-middle-class, white-picket-fence suburbanites in a place like Wisteria Lane, but we quickly become "bad" citizens *and* brown Others when socioeconomic status wavers a little. We are thinking of the Solis family in *Desperate Housewives* (2004–2012). When Carlos Solis (Ricardo Antonio Chavira) loses his job because he's blinded and becomes a massage therapist, the family is no longer privy to the country club's front entrance and must go around the back. The slope is slippery for Latinxs to become unwanted and bad citizens. With Gaby and Carlos this also transfers over to sexuality. They are not only hot for each other but also for others. Carlos discovers that Gaby is having an affair with their young Anglo gardener, John Rowland. At one point, they divorce, but this doesn't stop Gaby from jumping into bed with Carlos in a postdivorce affair.

We want to be fair here. Maybe the show is simply reconstructing real Latinx lives that do have problems—just like anyone else. The alternative is that Latinxs never appear in "bad" roles, as antagonists, as criminals, as unscrupulous individuals who are trying to take advantage of their surroundings and situation. Do Latinxs have extramarital affairs and file for divorce? Undoubtedly. In the case of *Desperate Housewives*, we are contending with the expectations of genre. It's not quite a soap opera, but it is heavily steeped in salacious behavior and sexual volatility. So if these sorts of behaviors do exist in the Latinx community—let's face it, they are not immune to such things—then why do we note it as significant? Are we too sensitive to certain representations on the screen? Is this a kind of fatigue we're articulating here? Rather than say that, yes, Latinxs sometimes do behave badly, we throw our popcorn at the screen and yell, "Not *another* instance of Latinxs being bad!"

Being "bad" also brings with it other forms of visible *difference*. In *Desperate Housewives*, Carlos develops an alcohol problem, and it's the Latina daughter, Juanita Solis (Madison De La Garza, Demi

Lovato's half sister), who is constantly dealing with weight issues. And there's some kind of sexual abuse in the family, too. Gabrielle murders her perverted stepfather, Alejandro Perez (Tony Plana). Of course, Latinxs cannot always be portrayed as chaste or pure. That's not who Latinxs are as a totality. We have all forms of behavior—the heroic and the horrible.

We don't necessarily take issue with Latinxs being portrayed as engaging in ethically questionable behavior. What we take issue with is the fact that these seem to be the *only* narratives circulated in film and TV. Let's take the case of *Breaking Bad* (2008–2013). We have a bad character, Walter White. Yet we don't hear any complaints that the white community is being stereotyped based on his role. There are just too many roles for white actors and the community they represent to be damaged by several roles that depict characters who embody the worst of humanity. This is narrative plentitude. We want this for Latinx *reel* representation.

Turning Upside Down Good versus Bad Latinxs

Robert Rodriguez flips the tradition of casting Jessica Alba as the celibate girl next door Latina by casting her as the assimilated, staid Latina turned pro-Latinx revolutionary in *Machete* (2010); he casts her against type, too, when he chooses her to play Irish stripper Nancy Callahan in *Sin City*. Rodriguez is playing up and critiquing precisely this good versus bad dichotomy that straightjackets Latinxs in mainstream media. Rodriguez knows how audiences have come to see her as playing particular characters. So he upsets that expectation by casting Alba in a role that is meant to defy what audiences think they already know about her. It shocks, but it also takes the viewer out of the neat and orderly organized mindset and into a world where things are no longer stable. Rodriguez, like his sometime partner in crime Quentin Tarantino, is notorious for taking actors we thought we knew and turning them into something we never would have expected.

Don't we need more of this kind of breaking of habituated ways of thinking about actors and film? One way is to take Latinx actors and cast them in roles that perhaps weren't written with a Latinx in mind. Such a move helps us deviate from those limited interpretations of how we see Latinxs on the screen, and it also helps prevent the sort of

Breacher (played by Danny Trejo) in *The Flash* (season 4, episode 4, 2017)

typecasting of Latinxs we've witnessed for decades. Yet we have actors like Danny Trejo, who seems to revel in repeating a similar character in everything from Robert Rodriguez films to commercials for Sling TV and Snickers.

He repeats this role in his cameo as Breacher in CW's *The Flash* (2014–) as the jealous *papá* of Gypsy, love interest to Cisco Ramone/Vibe. The constant return to the tattooed Latinx tough guy also gives him the opportunity to recast or reshape that somewhat stock character. Trejo, like the Alba example, is expected to play a Latinx assassin. Yet when he is cast as a similar-looking figure but instead in a comedic position such as the Snickers commercial, where he is Marsha Brady of *The Brady Bunch*, it made new our understanding of the roles Trejo tends to play. We feel this kind of fluidity in reimagining what the audience expects is a worthwhile endeavor and will have intriguing results if pursued.

We mentioned earlier Rodriguez's casting of the more mestizo-looking Danny Trejo as a radical move. Let's not forget that Danny Trejo's first forays into Hollywood cinema were in minor roles in films where he played characters with little to no dialogue and, quite literally, stock stereotypical roles. We first remember him quite clearly in the film *Blood In, Blood Out* as an inmate named Geronimo. He didn't have a line of dialogue in the film, but he certainly made an impression. But his big splash came in Rodriguez's *Desperado* (1995), where Trejo played the role of the knife-throwing assassin Navajas. Again, Trejo didn't say a single word, but he and Rodriguez used that for purposeful effect in the film. What Trejo and Rodriguez ended up doing was to take the stock Latinx stereotype, the kind of throwaway character Trejo was used to playing, and give it a more developed story line. That became *Machete*, which is what the character of Navajas in *Desperado* might have become if fully developed. Trejo seems ready made to play a Latinx stereotype—his tattoos are real, he has really served time in prison, and his face is not your typical leading man type of face. But now, as mentioned earlier, he has been able to play off of this stereotypical figure so that it transcends a film like *Desperado* and becomes a kind of cypher when he appears on screen, whether in feature films or in candy bar commercials.

Whether marked good or bad, the common denominator between Latinx and Latina is that we're visible in our extravagance—our *difference* from white, meritocratic, reasonable norms. That is certainly one of the appeals of having Latinx actors play Latinx characters. They provide an instant contrast both culturally and visually. Unfortunately, this sets Latinxs up for playing against the norm in contrast to the protagonist. Think of Marvel's *Ant-Man* (2015) and its sequel, *Ant-Man and the Wasp* (2018). The protagonist and title character of the first film, played by Paul Rudd, is literally a convicted criminal, and the opening scene reveals that he's in prison. But he has a close friend who also dabbles in criminality—named, simply, Luis. Michael Peña plays this sidekick to the hilt, and he steals most of the scenes in which he appears. Rudd and Peña have played many comedic roles in their careers, and they are quite adept at it. Yet Peña's sole purpose in the film, seemingly, is to provide the sort of difference we're noting—he *contrasts* Rudd throughout the film. At one point in the sequel, Peña's character drives a car with painted flames and, at one point, practically begs for a superhero suit, even one without powers. Interestingly, imagine what would happen if we reversed the actors playing these roles so that Peña was the Ant-Man and Rudd played "Louis." We suspect some Latinx studies scholars would be riled that Peña played a criminal, which is stereotypical of Latinxs. Yet that isn't what is mentioned when Rudd is Ant-Man. Latinxs are still cast in minor, stereotypical roles, and truly substantive roles are all too few and far between. Latinxs are often used as a difference marker. We want Latinxs to be more than that.

Reel Reconstructions that Matter and a Wrap-Up

We have a president of the United States in 2018 who, in his first conference to announce his candidacy, proclaimed that Mexicans were murderers, rapists, drug dealers, and that when Mexico sends their citizens to the United States, they are not sending their best. This viewpoint, which should not be a mainstream view, is the position of the highest office in the United States. Is it any wonder where Donald Trump would get such an idea, the inveterate TV watcher that he is? African Americans and Latinxs are always marked with the specter of criminality thanks to laziness in thinking, lack of firsthand knowledge or extensive experience, and blatant stereotypes that we encounter in the media. And now, thanks in large measure to the fallout of the 9/11 terrorist attacks in the United States in 2001, minorities who do commit violence become an example of widespread violence within that particular group thanks to the confirmation bias. It is a verifiable fact that when a man killed in the name of Islam in perversion of one of the three major Abrahamic faiths on this planet, President Trump wasted little time in bemoaning the murderous intent of "radical Islam." Yet when white male shooters murdered dozens in Las Vegas and in a small-town church in Texas and a high school in Parkland, Florida, we were offered "thoughts and prayers."

We end this chapter by reminding our readers that reel reconstructions of Latinxs as bad subjects are part of a pattern that reveals the way certain minority groups are thought of in the United States. That should tell us at least two things. First, representations do, in fact, matter. When the U.S. president gets much of his information from TV, media and media representation matter more than ever. Second, not only should film and TV media get better, it is imperative that they get better in how they represent Latinxs.

YESTERDAY'S AND TODAY'S REEL BAD HOMBRES

Schrödinger's Latinx: Silver-Screen Origins of Our Absent-Presence and Present-Absence

In the last chapter, we mentioned several foundational reels that set the machinery in motion for the way the silver-screen-reconstructed Latinxs are at once present, then absent in our presence as well as absent, but then present in our absence. Here we will dig deeper into the *bad* part of this equation in all its discomforting—and *threatening*—permutations: from no-good layabouts to shoot-'em-up pistoleros and gangbangers.

Let's return our critical lens to one such foundational film, D. W. Griffith's twelve-reel behemoth *Birth of a Nation* (1915). For its day, the film was a remarkable technical achievement. Griffith was able to take his enormous camera equipment places not seen before. He had an extraordinary eye for framing artful mise-en-scènes. However, for all of its technical achievement, it fell more than short in content. This film is a case where we see radical innovation in the form of telling but a lazy, careless building of content. As D. W. Griffith's camera panned left to right, and before it settled on its images that glorify the Aryan nation, Mexicans were mostly portrayed as layabouts.

Griffith takes the stereotypical myths of the day and projects them backward, reversing time's arrow to make it appear as if the wish fulfillment of white supremacy were not only a reality but predetermined. The white figures are destined to be leaders and captains of industry, while brown peoples are characterized exactly as the racist sees them. The film is extraordinary for giving us an unexpurgated window into the thoughts and ideals of a racist. It is silver screen's manifest destiny that justifies the collateral damage—the obliteration—of brown subjects in the inevitable expansion and forward march of whiteness.

Of course, Griffith did not create ex nihilo the stereotype of the lazy Mexican. Such a figure was already propagated in the imagination of white America through other forms of entertainment and reporting. The significance of Griffith's film, or at least one significance, is that it put the stereotype in a dynamic visual format that had never been seen before.

Caricatures of minorities had long appeared in print media, but this was different. Film, for all its multimodality, is visually dominant. It requires no mediation between the image and the audience. There are no words to be interpreted, as in the reading of a novel. The visual impression a stereotyped character made in the early days of cinema must have been massive. Even today, with what we must surely admit are much more sophisticated audiences than those who watched *Birth of a Nation* for the first time, we know that representation does indeed matter.

Griffith's technical skill and achievement took colloquial knowledge and understandings of the United States by white people and concretized them in the dynamic visual medium of film. This is what makes the film so execrable when we see the harm it does for people who are other than white men. A shoddy product may have been laughable, so we would then have sorry form *and* defamatory content, leading to an easily dismissible film. But the quality of the film, for its time, is outstanding. Thus, the technical execution then lends its own credibility and ethos to the content.

We think it's apt to compare *Birth of a Nation* with Leni Riefenstahl's *Triumph of the Will* (1935)—also arguably an extraordinary accomplishment in terms of its aesthetic composition; she took the camera eye to new extraordinary heights, literally, with her epic aerial shots of the Nazi soldiers marching in unison. In the end, though, the aesthetic gives shape to racist propaganda. Both films offer aesthetically pleasing visual experiences. However, they function more like paeans (love epistles?) to the myth of white supremacy.

Ultimately, we can't separate form from content. It's a gestalt experience. So, even though we have an excellence of execution, the wretched race propaganda and risible nationalism of fascist ideologies deform these silver-screen narratives of race. We have to have our critical eyes wide open with these films of yesteryear and today (think about the incredible technical innovations of *Avatar* that envelope the age-old white-savior myth) because the more technically brilliant, the more that audiences might be wowed; the grandeur, majesty, and sublimity of these films make racism pretty.

While it's unfortunate that these films were made and likely will continue to be made, we don't think the solution is censorship. We believe in total freedom when it comes to the making of cultural phenomena, but in freedom that's grounded in a deep responsibility to the subject matter being reconstructed—and this especially when a given film or TV product makes explicit claims to factual representation.

With *Birth of a Nation* and *Triumph of the Will* we could have a permanent chyron that says that the ideology is complete garbage but the composition of the film is worth looking at. Censorship is a wrong step in the other direction.

We cannot censor within the bounds of legality. Now, the laws for what is obscene are for lawyers and politicians and judges. Rather, we must continue to welcome the creation of films and media even if we disagree with or dislike them. We are human, so there are certainly films we would rather not waste our time on. There are films that are made by political groups that are meant to frighten or anger political constituents or to stir up hatred. We would like to banish these into oblivion. But that is censorship. What we *can* do is review such a film and flay it for all to see. Of course, there are those who will get drunk on such propaganda no matter how much we tell them it's not worth their time.

In the end, and this is the *why* of this book, we need to be aware of all the elements that make up film and TV narratives so we can understand exactly how they reconstruct (for better or worse) Latinx identities and experiences. It's why we have to critically interrogate and pull apart films like *Birth of a Nation* and not dismiss them out of hand—or censor them altogether. We can't ignore these films. They exist in the world. And what they have done will be used to the same effect if we, as critics, do not become razors that slice and dissect the interplay between design and ideology.

Birth of a Nation as Progenitor of America's Racialized Modern Consciousness

Some argue that Harriet Beecher Stowe's *Uncle Tom's Cabin* (1852) started the U.S. Civil War. Given that some two hundred million people have seen *Birth of a Nation*, one could argue that it created our modern racialized consciousness. Let's not forget that *Birth of a Nation* was adapted from a 1905 novel by Thomas F. Dixon titled *The Clansman: A Historical Romance of the Ku Klux Klan*. While there's plenty of room for disagreeing with the idea that Stowe's novel started the Civil War, it is a fact that Dixon's book led directly to *Birth of a Nation*. So, in a way, *The Clansman* can be seen as starting (continuing?) a war for the right of white supremacy to be the dominant ideology of the United States.

We have to pull back, however, on the argument that the film created our modern racialized consciousness. White supremacy was well on its way to be the natural state of affairs in this country even before it was founded as an independent nation. The Founding Fathers knew the abolition of slavery had to happen, but Hamilton, Washington, Jefferson, and Madison (the latter three Southerners and slave owners) also realized that it was an impossibility for them to try to codify the illegality of slavery in the nation's founding documents. So they thought that later generations would take up the issue and handle it the best way they could. It seems the Founding Fathers had too much faith in the generations that followed.

Birth of a Nation turned white supremacy into a neatly packaged, consumable, transportable myth for the United States. That is the power of it, and many viewers have been susceptible to its seduction. In the end, however, it is incumbent on those who find such ideologies abhorrent to deride it and lay it low at every opportunity we get. We cannot do this if we seal up all copies in a time capsule until the nation can handle it. In this sense, what *Birth of a Nation* did create was an occasion to detail its perversity and lack of imagination.

Filmic Imaginaries Matter, and in Many Directions of Influence

Do films and TV change people's attitudes and behaviors, or do they simply reflect and reconstruct what's already out there? We're of the position that inspiration and motivation can come from any and all places and may take any and all forms. We mention this earlier in the book, but it's worth restating here: we are not passive absorptive sponges. We metabolize all of culture and reconstruct it in new and innovative ways. So, while there continue to be films and TV shows today that operate like *Birth of a Nation*, we are also sophisticated consumers of this cultural phenomenon. In other words, why assume such cultural phenomena only changes or shapes minds in one direction? It's just as likely that in our active metabolizing of them we are driven to think and act in a completely different way than the film or TV show intends. *← out of no thing*

Racist films and TV shows are not created ex nihilo. They build on what already exists within the creator (and creator as viewer), which is a product of what exists in the world. Put another way, *Birth of a Nation* would not exist in a world free of white supremacy. These films are not the spark in the world, but they are the vehicle for whatever insights or ideologies already exist within the viewer.

Latinx Silver-Screen Origins and Black Masks

In 1920, Douglas Fairbanks dons a black mask in *The Mark of Zorro*—and the background Latinx campesinos seem to perpetually nap under whatever tree or roof overhang presents itself. In so doing, this silver-

screen reconstruction of Latinxs creates links between class and race: nineteenth-century Californio hacendados like Don Diego Vega/Zorro (Fairbanks in brownface) are seen as active and the agents of change. Unlike the lazy campesinos, Don Diego Vega doesn't seem to sleep at all, performing his dandy rituals by day and swashbuckling as Zorro by night. While it perpetuates stereotypes of the lazy campesino, it's one of the first—if not *the* first—film to bring a class dimension into the reconstruction of Latinx identities and experiences. And, of course, for as much as we see the Latinx

Zorro (played by Douglas Fairbanks) in *The Mark of Zorro* (1920)

gentry class intermingle (slumming it with a mask) with the working-class Latinxs, in the end the film etches into stone that Manichean ideology inherited from Euro-Spanish conquistadores: light-skinned criollos are inherently better (civilized) than dark-skinned mestizos (uncivilized).

Tyrone Power's various Zorro iterations, along with the comic-book spin-offs, continued to perpetuate this criollo as savior versus mestizo as hapless imaginary. Yet as we already mentioned, we aren't passive absorptive sponges. Zorro has proved to be an important superhero for many Latinxs. This is where we would like to parse the savior myth from the idea of a superhero. The white-savior myth is not necessarily a superhero myth, but they both have in common the idea that the savior or the hero has access to power that the common folk, the people who are in need, find unattainable. It is the whiteness of the white savior that allows him or her to gain access to power structures or upend prejudicial status quo policies. A superhero's access isn't necessarily a function of his or her whiteness, though a wide majority of the early superheroes in comics were white (Batman) or were foreign born but seen as white (Superman, Wonder Woman). Later superheroes of color exemplify what we're articulating here. Their power manifests in spite of whiteness.

Through much of the history of the United States, people of color have had little recourse for resolving oppressive policies or conditions on their own. Solidarity during the time of American slavery would get everyone lynched, mutilated, beaten, raped, or some combination of all of these. Historically, people of color have not had the means with which to save themselves. And despite the advancements for people of color during the push for and as a consequence of civil rights, one might argue that some minority communities still cannot attain justice or equal treatment without the intervention of white allies. It is really unsurprising that films propagate what has been a historical trend. It is not absolute; there are instances where people of color were able to help themselves. But relatively speaking, these occur a very small percentage of the time across the broad swath of this nation's history.

Zorro is the smartest landed gentry of them all. He ingratiates the campesinos by giving them money robbed from the rich, but they in turn work the crops that sustain his hacienda and decadent lifestyle.

He's not quite Robin Hood. Maybe he robs from the rich and gives to the poor so that the poor will leave him and his lavish hacienda alone. On the other hand, don't we all like a little bit of the bad hombre in superheroes like Zorro? Batman's motivation is made crystal clear, and every reboot of Batman reminds us how forever altered Bruce is after witnessing the murders of his father and mother. Zorro is not traumatized to positive action for the greater good. Maybe he is just keeping the peasants happy and the bourgeoisie full of angst. Either way, Zorro turns out to be heroic, and so it's no wonder that, as kids, many of us Latinxs wanted to be like him. He is a figure of vigilante justice who skirts around the established (and unfair) laws to serve a higher sense of justice.

So, while Zorro works from within a criollo privilege, maybe we shouldn't hold this against him. Indeed, maybe we should reevaluate his role in our lives and see how he modeled the way privilege can be used for social good. Zorro uses his education (one well paid for) on behalf of those who cannot achieve fairness and justice on their own.

Zorro's Many Masks

Even with the civil rights and brown power movements in the rear-view mirror of history, Zorro continued to capture imaginations and perpetuate a *casta* ideology: upper-class criollo Latinxs as smart and able versus working-class mestizos as dumb and in need. This contin-ues in Martin Campbell's 1998 reboot, *The Mask of Zorro*, where the English-accented Anthony Hopkins is cast as the wizened Zorro and An-tonio Banderas plays the new generation of Zorro as Alejan-dro Murrieta—the fictional brother of Joaquin Murrieta, one of our great Latinx histor-ical heroes.

Don Diego de la Vega (played by Anthony Hopkins) in *The Mask of Zorro* (1998)

What we see is an in-teresting mix of old-school Hollywood (white actors in brownface) and the newer impulse to diversify (somewhat) with the inclusion of a female coprotagonist, Catherine Zeta-Jones as the Latina Elena Montero. With two of the three prominent Latinx characters played by actors with Spanish accents (of Welsh ancestry), maybe the studio thought it could fool viewers into thinking of them as Latinx. Of course, we're not fooled. But we also have to think about Hollywood's bottom line: money.

The studios cast stars to get people into theater seats. And, remember, *The Mask of Zorro* was released in 1998. Latinas who had appeared in films in the 1980s, like María Chonchita Alonzo, may have been seen as too old (as ludicrous as that is). One might have expected Salma Hayek in the role—opposite her costar from *Desperado*, Antonio Banderas—but she wasn't cast. Were there other actresses of Latinx heritage who might have been cast? Absolutely. We might ask the same of U.S. Latino actors. Who else might the filmmakers have cast in Antonio Banderas's place? At the time, he was a rising star—his huge breakthrough with *Desperado*—but as in the case with Hayek and Penélope Cruz, what other Latinos could have been cast in *Mask of Zorro*? Jimmy Smits or Edward James Olmos, the go-to Latino stars? Perhaps Benjamin Bratt? But the studio producers want sure things, and at the time a Smits or Olmos or Bratt didn't seem to present this possibility.

If Robert Rodriguez had helmed *Mask of Zorro*, as he was asked but then declined, we probably wouldn't be having this discussion. Outside the studio system, Rodriguez can and does take so-called risks, and at all levels, including casting. He probably wouldn't have done what was done, to reboot a film that features Latinxs down to the very DNA of the story world but where no U.S. Latinxs are cast.

The Western Redux

Zorro's part of a much larger white/criollo savior to hapless Latino/ manifest destiny mythos. The genre that seemed to deepen and spread wide this mythos has to be the Western. The great *pensador* Wittgenstein loved his Westerns. The clear-cut good versus evil Manichean formula put his brain to rest. But, as we discussed in the last chapter concerning John Wayne and John Ford, within this good (white cowboy) versus evil (Latinx bandito), the U.S. Western cemented in place a Latinx racialized imaginary. If Native Americans or

Latinxs got in the way of white-coded progress and expansion, then it was open season. Sergio Leone's spaghetti Westerns depict the white protagonist (Eastwood) as a taciturn, mysterious badass who ends up gunslinging in U.S.-Mexican border towns where Latinxs are either helpless campesinos or slobberingly despicable villains. These white heroes tend to have Latinx senoritas hanging on their arms. For instance, in *A Fistful of Dollars*, "The Man with No Name" (Eastwood) uses his smarts and sharpshooting skills to take out the Rojo brothers, Don Miguel and Esteban and Ramón, to save Marisol, the Latina damsel in distress. She asks, "Why do you do this for us?" And recall the Man with No Name in Leone's *The Good, the Bad, and the Ugly* (1966), where the white guy is good and the ugly is Latinx: the fast-talking, crude, buffoon bandito, Tuco "The Rat" Benedicto Pacífico Juan María Ramírez.

Although Eastwood's character, interestingly enough, is known as the "Man with No Name," he is called by several names in the trilogy of films that bears this designation. He is "Joe" in *A Fistful of Dollars*, "Monco" in *For a Few Dollars More*, and "Blondie" in *The Good, the Bad, and the Ugly*. Blondie isn't really good, just as Tuco isn't really ugly. Lee Van Cleef, who plays Angel Eyes, isn't bad. Rather, he's an opportunist (not at the level of the other two) and a man who wants to win. Despite the clearly defined categories of the film's title, the characters are all really just variations of the same thing, changed

Tuco Benedicto Pacífico Juan María Ramírez, aka "The Rat" (played by Eli Wallach) in *The Good, the Bad, and the Ugly* (1966)

by circumstance, opportunity, and talent. And while Eli Wallach is in brownface (as are most of the Italian actors who are playing Latinxs in the film), his performance is a revelation. He has the most dialogue, he carries most of the film, which is two minutes shy of three hours, and he is much more complex than his "rat" designation indicates. He also has the greatest emotional spectrum of any character in *The Good, the Bad, and the Ugly*. He distrusts Blondie, but he builds a kind of friendship of opportunity with him. We see him left for dead in the desert, the reason unknown but what certainly looks like Blondie's caprice or sadism. Tuco has a heartrending reunion with his estranged brother, now a priest, at the mission where Blondie convalesces. And he is again psychologically tortured until the very last minutes of the film.

We do not see the explicitly marked white savior in the West on film until John Sturges's *The Magnificent Seven* (1966), with its seven heroes (well, six plus the Irish Mexican–identified character, Bernardo O'Reilly) who save an entire village of helpless Latinxs. There's that scene when, standing with sombreros in hand, the campesinos ask in truncated, heavily accented English, "We wish you to help us." The magnificent seven white saviors take down the crazed Mexican, Calvera (played yet again by Eli Wallach in brownface).

And then a decade later, in a film such as *The Outlaw Josey Wales* (1976), we have a Confederate "good guy"; indeed, the film was based on the novel of the same name by Forrest Carter, a man known for his expressed support of white supremacy and the KKK. Carter was

Mexican farmers make their plea to Cajun mercenary Chris Adams (played by Yul Brynner) in *The Magnificent Seven* (1960)

named after Nathan Bedford Forrest, founder of the KKK and the subject of *Birth of a Nation*. Later still, we have Kevin Costner's *Dances with Wolves* and Eastwood again in the Oscar-winning *Unforgiven* (1992) playing Will Munny, who avenges the murder of his black friend (Morgan Freeman) and saves a town and a group of women from another vengeful white man (Gene Hackman).

Of course, this is all silver-screen reconstruction. We know, however, from actual historical events that during this time in history, there was only genocide of Mexicans and Native Americans. There were no white saviors for many victims of whites during the push for manifest destiny. It was more like white executioners, sanctioned by the U.S. Army and government. In other words, Leone takes up the Western as portrayed by Ford and others. He and these filmmakers weren't making documentaries. There is no devotion to facts in their work. Leone isn't even filming in the American West, and the vast majority of his actors are Italians speaking in Italian. Leone takes up the already established tradition of the myth of the American West as represented in the Western genre of American cinema.

There's George Stevens's *Giant* (1956), which takes the tropes of the Western and refashions them as a dynastic epic, with a number of progressive (surprising for the epoch) elements. First, the white patriarch is played by a gay actor, Rock Hudson. Second, this white patriarch, Jordan "Bick" Benedict, defends Mexicans in a café owned by Sarge (Mickey Simpson), a part clearly scripted as a white-racist bigot. Third, the striking image of Bick's mixed-race Latino-Anglo grandson ends the film. This single image retroactively undermines all of the white-racist privilege that has come before.

We see the roots of *Giant* growing into a film like *Lone Star* (1996). Here John Sayles peels back the skin on white patriarchy, revealing how Sheriff Buddy Deeds isn't driven so much by reason as all in the town come to believe but rather murderous unreason. As his affairs and the murdered bodies pile up, so, too, does the image of the white patriarchal savior come tumbling down. The path out of all this for his son is to embrace fully his love for the Latina Pilar (Elizabeth Peña)—his half sister. Sayles subverts the white-savior figure so common in film. The sins of the father are only absolved by the son's turning away from hatred and embracing the Other, of which he is now a part.

Latinxs (Brownface or Otherwise) Last on and First Off

As it tends to happen in Hollywood, in any given mercenary posse, the Latinxs are the first to go. We see this with Bernardo O'Reilly in *The Magnificent Seven* and in more recent films with multicultural packs of mercenaries. Later we see it with Christopher Cain's *Young Guns* (1988), when Lou Diamond Phillips as the vision-questing, knife-throwing Jose Chavez y Chavez is the first to be killed off. When Hollywood's writing and casting began to become more diverse, whiteness continued to hang like an amulet of great power. And this is across all film genres. Think of George Romero's groundbreaking film *Night of the Living Dead* (1968), where both the black man and white woman survive the zombies. Well, it's the black man who is shot and killed by a white policeman who "thought" he was a zombie. Or think of *Alien* (1979), when Sigourney Weaver's Ripley is the last survivor of the ship *Nostromo*, but the rest of the crew, and Yaphet Kotto's Parker, die. The alien itself is literally black and is portrayed in a suit by a black man.

This history of the white survivor (we don't simply have white-savior syndrome!) is so entrenched, it's ripe for satire. That is exactly why Jordan Peele's Oscar-winning *Get Out* (2017) works so brilliantly. Throughout the entire film, the audience is primed to expect the black protagonist, Chris Washington, played by Daniel Kaluuya, not to survive through the end of the film. The films we mention came decades before Peele's film. But long histories sometimes become recent histories.

In our reconstructing a Latinx film history that works within and against the Manichaeanism at the heart of the Western genre, we have to mention Sam Peckinpah's *Bring Me the Head of Alfredo Garcia* (1974). Peckinpah energetically uses and abuses tropes seen in Westerns such as *The Searchers* and John Huston's *The Treasure of the Sierra Madre*. It still features a white savior (Warren Oates as Bennie) who saves the Latina damsel in distress (Isla Vega as Elita), but it locates the bad in privilege and whiteness: the hacendado known as El Jefe (Emilio Fernández) and the marauding white bikers headed by Kris Kristofferson who gang rape Elita. Peckinpah's film, while still limited in the ways we mentioned, does feature breakthroughs of textured characters.

Bring Me the Head of Alfredo Garcia is probably the starting point on the journey of realizing the kinds of stories featuring Latinxs that are portrayed in films such as *From Dusk till Dawn* (1996). In *From Dusk till Dawn*, Rodriguez makes explicit links to the Western, among other genres, to play up and against the Western savior myth. There's George Clooney as Seth Gecko, who drives away after a night of vampire destruction. But there's also Harvey Keitel as Jacob Fuller, who exaggeratedly embodies the white-savior role as a pastor, and the Latinxs turned vamps take him out. Moreover, it's not Clooney driving into the sunset that ends the film. It is an image of the Titty Twister bar from behind, showing that the bar/nightclub where all the vampire action took place was only a modern facade of the tip of a Mesoamerican pyramid that descends into a huge crater. Rodriguez plants the seeds for alternative mythos: the mixed-race Latinx created out of the violence and rape by the conquistadores evolved today into transmogrifying vamps that fight back.

New Sheep's Clothes and Wrap-Up

While yesteryear's Westerns are now largely extinct, they seem to be appearing in disguise in other genres—and with the Manichaean allegory fully intact. Indeed, like genres over time generally, yesteryear's overtly offensive, stereotypical Westerns would no longer make money at the box office. They continue to exist, but in less obviously offensive ways. Consider *Dances with Wolves* again. In the golden age of the Western, every single Native American character would have been played by a non-Native actor. We would not have seen such care taken to capture Native languages somewhat accurately. And when we did have the unadorned white-savior myth, it came in the shape of Michael Douglas as unemployed defense engineer William Foster in *Falling Down* (1993).

The moment of white resurrection happens in and through his journey through Latinx East L.A. In many ways Douglas/Foster in *Falling Down* was a precursor of today's alt-right in the United States—those who go on and on about "white genocide" as if the inclusion of diverse actors is equal to the sorts of genocide white groups have engaged in throughout world history.

William Foster (played by Michael Douglas) with "Gang Member" (played by Agustin Rodriguez) in *Falling Down* (1993)

The Latinx pistolero now appears regularly in TV's narco dramas. In the 1980s, Latinxs got a pistolero makeover with *Miami Vice* (1984–1989), which had everybody wearing pastel tees and white suit jackets a la Tubbs and "Sonny" Crocket. That show played against all sorts of stories of Latinx drug lords and gangbangers, including Colombian drug dealer Calderone, played by the Nuyorican playwright and poet Miguel Piñero. The series nearly had a more interesting portrayal of a Latinx who wasn't a drug kingpin. In the show's pilot, the creators introduced Eddie Rivera (played by Jimmy Smits), poised to become Sonny's sidekick and not Tubbs. It opened with Sonny asking if he'd done the "hot-blooded machismo number and stomped out of the house." Eddie: "No wife of mine out to work for a living." In addition to the thick accent, he had the mandatory cross on a necklace to remind us that he's Catholic. As has become the tradition, a sustained, complex Latinx character doesn't last long. Eddie, along with Jimmy Smits's nuanced acting, was blown to oblivion within the first eleven minutes of the first episode.

In 2003, NBC aired the flash-in-the-pan, six-episode series *Kingpin*. Here Latinxs were portrayed as either shooting each other, doing and/or pushing drugs, or feeding human appendages to pet tigers. The creators wrote into the story the character Ernesto (played by Jacob Vargas). He's wildly irrational and glaringly crass, sporting a garish gold medallion, ornate cowboy hat, and coiled whip. He's portrayed as a man-child who lives lavishly in a Liberace-style mansion. He is chock full of hot-tempered flashes and violent acts. He's calmed down only by the paternal embrace of the clean-cut (and Caucasian featured), Ivy League–educated Miguel Cadena (played by Colombian Puerto Rican Yancey Arias). The creators set him in stark contrast to Vargas. As opposed to Ernesto's crass kingpin ways, Miguel uses more respectable, corporate-savvy means to kill people. He uses his Harvard-educated smarts to infiltrate new drug markets. *Kingpin* is the Western in new clothing. It's also TV trying to tap into a Latinx market but not knowing how to do it and not taking the time and effort to learn. The writers and show creators imagined what the Latinx drug world *might* be like based on the little that they saw in headlines and in other areas of popular culture. It's as if they realized, "Latinxs watch a lot of TV! Let's make a Latinx drama!" And TV keeps at it with *Narcos* (2015–), *Queen of the South* (2016–), *The Bridge* (2013–2014), and all those narco dramas built in and around real murderous figures such as El Chapo Guzmán and Pablo Escobar.

In 2008, we had the start of *Breaking Bad*, a show that ran until 2013. While creator Vince Gilligan represented a greater array of Latinx types (certainly more than *Sicario*) as smart and as dark and light (Jesse's girlfriend Andrea Cantillo, for instance), this was probably demographic reality forcing Gilligan's hand. From main roles to extras, how can you *not* cast Latinxs when setting a narrative in the Latinx-dominant region of Albuquerque, New Mexico? This said, there was some innovation in *Breaking Bad*. Latinx characters appear in recurring roles, including Latinx Drug Enforcement Administration agent Steven Gomez (Steven Michael Quezada). He does his job effectively and puts up with his insensitive partner and friend, Hank Schrader (Dean Norris), who calls him "Gomie." And Gilligan doesn't set Gomez up as the good Latinx to cardboard cutout Latinx bad characters. The casting of Giancarlo Esposito as the visibly Afro-Latino Gustavo "Gus" Fring is significant—and he's probably the smartest guy in the show. He's never ruffled, even when running a legit fast-food business, Los Pollos Hermanos, as cover for growing a vast drug empire. Indeed, Gus is arguably a more interesting character than Walter *White*—who just barely manages to outwit Gus. This said, the white protagonist wins in the end. And so we're going to be critical. But what if this had been Walter *Brown*, a drug kingpin played by a Latinx actor? We'd likely be as critical. If it's a white protagonist and Latinx supporting cast, it's bad. But if it's a Latinx protagonist with moral relativism issues, it's bad. It's a conversation that requires nuance, which is what we're doing with this book.

With the narco-drama narratives produced in abundance, the Western has been transformed—and with it the representation of Latinxs, for better or worse. Think *Sicario* and Benicio del Toro's turn in that film. He's got a bit of the outlaw and vigilante in him, but he also has an ethical sense of what is right. However, the film ends with audiences thinking mostly about the white, naive protagonist Kate Macer (Emily Blunt), menaced by del Toro playing the sociopathic Alejandro. It's the white/good versus brown/bad Western all dressed up in new clothes.

And there's *Sons of Anarchy* (2008–2014), which dares to do more with its creation of the character Juice. The show's writers give him smarts.

Juan Carlos "Juice" Ortiz (played by Theo Rossi) in *Sons of Anarchy* (season 7, episode 7, 2014)

Juice is in charge of the club's intelligence and has computer-hacking skills. But he's also the most tragic figure in the show, stemming from his passing as Latinx in order to hide his African American bloodline. His paranoia leads him to think and behave in ways that make him constantly suspicious to the others. Yet in the end Juice winds up being the tragic mulatto figure. The consequences of Juice's passing as Latinx result in his becoming the submissive "bottom" to a white Aryan nation gang in prison. And his passing as Latinx ultimately leads to the accumulation of lies that creates mass murderous mayhem of Asians, Blacks, Latinxs, and whites at the show's end. He's cast into the worst possible situation because he is fated never to belong to any group, just like all tragic mulattoes in literature and film.

In the final two seasons of *Sons of Anarchy*, something truly innovative happens with the introduction of the character Nero Padilla, played by Jimmy Smits. He's bad Latinx—as are pretty much all the characters in the show. His business, Diosa International, is built on the exploitation of women as prostitutes, and he runs the Latinx gang the ByzLats. As the story unfolds, he becomes less and less the macho, gangbanger patriarch and more the comforting, thinking companion (Gemma) and friend (Jax). In the end, he gets out of the life to be able to take care of his disabled son, Lucius Padilla (Gybby Eusebio). He comes into a Latinx masculinity that's not seen often on TV. Of course, this is not entirely new. As of this writing, the *Sons of Anarchy* Latinx spin-off, *Mayans*, is set to debut on FX. We hope for more complexity in the characterization of the Latinx community in the series.

We saw a glimmer of this new Latinx masculinity in Gregory Nava's *My Family*, when, at the end of the film, Jimmy Smits (as the character Jimmy) overcomes his anger issues grown from his brother's murder and later his wife's death during childbirth. He makes amends with his estranged son, Carlitos. He shifts gears from angry Latinx to a Latinx who embraces a masculinity that allows for the shedding of tears and confession of deep love. And in Edward James Olmos's *American Me* (1992) we see the protagonist, Santana (Edward James Olmos), come to realize how his *machista* ways contribute to the genocide of his people. His tragic end comes as a result of his realization that he wants to embrace a new Latino masculinity and discard an internalized, Euro-Spaniard colonial supermacho mentality.

Of course, we know when Latinxs are able to shape stories of Latinxs and of Latinx culture, we get intriguing, complex, nuanced stories and characterization. But we don't expect this in shows like *Sons of Anarchy*. As much as Juice slips into old paradigms, Nero opens up new ways of seeing Latinx pistoleros—and with this, constructions of Latinx masculinity.

Chapter 3

LAUGHING *MATTERS*

First There Was Speedy

How did Speedy Gonzales, with his "Ándale! ¡Ándale! ¡Arriba! ¡Arriba! ¡Epa! ¡Epa! ¡Epa! Yeehaw!" become the signifier for all Latinxs? If we are being truly accurate, Speedy is a Mexican national, not a U.S. Latinx— which is silly because we're discussing an anthropomorphic mouse. He's sly and always quick with a joke. He outwits everyone and is "the fastest mouse in all of Mexico." He is an animated stereotype, just like Pepe le Pew, Foghorn Leghorn, or Bugs Bunny.

Speedy was brought to life in large measure because of Mel Blanc—remembered as one of the greatest cartoon voice actors who ever lived. But before he was known for Bugs and Speedy and the rest of the Warner Brothers characters, he was a regular performer on *The Jack Benny Program* on radio and later on TV. His signature character, "Sy, the Little Mexican," was so reductionist, he was literally mono-syllabic, saying "Sí" or similar variants in response to questions and prompts from Benny's "straight man" character. Many of us have seen those comedic routines and wonder what makes them so hilarious. The audience is figuratively dying with laughter. But when you hear Blanc's burdensome Spanish accent, you can hear Speedy Gonzales in rudimentary fashion. Blanc was known as "the man with a thousand voices," but some of them, such as Speedy's and Pepe's voices, are grossly stereotypical and not good at all. The bad impression is part of the gag. Animation, in visuals and in vocals, has been founded on simple stereotypes. William Nericcio has extensively explored the implications of Speedy Gonzales and the persistence of Mexican stereotypes in the United States.

Speedy is cut exactly from the same sort of cloth as Griffith's stereotypes that we discussed in the last chapter. Speedy is the "good guy" in the shorts that feature him as protagonist. The mouse, the ostensible prey, is almost always the "good guy" in these animated

Speedy Gonzales and in Looney Tunes "Tabasco Road" (1957)

shorts, which is why Itchy and Scratchy on *The Simpsons* are so brilliant. The show within a show overturns this trope and has the mouse, Itchy, as the architect of some truly horrible tortures wreaked on the cat, Scratchy. In terms of Speedy, having him as the good guy makes the audience root for him. Yet doesn't that have the adverse effect of making his stereotypical features "good"? It's all a bit insidious. Speedy is a hero, and his whole affect and characterization seem sanctioned for the good. In effect, it's okay that Speedy is a stereotype because he's one of the "good" Mexicans.

Latinx Shuckin' and Jivin'

In the mid- to late 1970s, ABC TV introduced prime-time viewers to Latinx characters with *Chico and the Man* (1974–1978) and *Welcome Back, Kotter* (1975–1979). They did so with different means and goals. *Chico and the Man* was unambiguously Latinx—in its setting and development of the Latinx *communidad*. And it was a ratings draw. Here we have a Latinx character, *played by a Latinx actor*, speaking truth to power on the small screen. Freddie Prinze as Francisco "Chico" Rodriguez, who constantly foregrounded his Mexican and Hungarian ancestry, was extraordinarily innovative.

In between his grumpy white boss's racist invectives, Chico would throw down some politically charged, satirical lines. When "The Man" makes a crack about Chico being Latinx, and therefore lazy, Chico responds by telling The Man how he got his silver star in Vietnam. There are many other moments in *Chico and the Man* when Prinze dares to use caustic and socially pointed humor—and this was back in the mid- to late 1970s. That's why Prinze's suicide is all the more lamentable. It is hard not to think of what might have been had *Chico and the Man* continued with Prinze as the title character. Freddie Prinze suffered

Chico Rodriguez (played by Freddie Prinze) in *Chico and the Man* (season 2, episode 11, 1975)

from depression and an addiction to quaaludes. Some attribute this to his inability to handle his sudden rise to fame after his Johnny Carson appearance. Perhaps it was being Latinx and an inability finally to reconcile his use of a comic buffoon type to destabilize Latinx stereotypes. Only twenty-two years old, he shot himself three years after his first appearance on the *Tonight Show* and only three years into *Chico and the Man*. The show was clearly generating significant ratings, and it would be many years before another successful TV show would engage in that way with substantive Latinidad.

In contrast, in *Welcome Back, Kotter*, with its ensemble cast and only a few minority representatives, diversity was tokenized. The character Juan Luis Pedro Felipo de Huevos Epstein (played brilliantly by Robert Hegyes, of Hungarian and Italian ancestry), known simply as Epstein, was envisioned as an intriguing amalgam of Puerto Rican and Jewish heritage. So even in a show that featured token characters, not all actors aligned with the ethnicity of the characters they portrayed.

We see this same tokenizing more recently as well. Take Fez (Wilmer Valderama) in *That '70s Show* (1998–2006), who was portrayed as an oversexed buffoon chock full of malapropisms. And there is the thick-Spanish-accented Rico who appeared in *King of Queens* (1998–2007) as a kind of punching bag for the show's racialized and sexualized jokes. And, while we're not sure it was meant to be comical, there is the episode of *Glee* (February 7, 2012) when singer Ricky Martin plays the role of Spanish teacher David Martinez, who breaks out into song and dance routines for "Sexy and I Know It" and "La Isla Bonita." In the skit "Jewelry Party" on *Saturday Night Live*, Cecily Strong brownfaces a caricature of Sofía Vergara, playing up her over-the-top English accent and ignorance—she's dating a misogynist and doesn't know it. Caricaturing in brownface already caricatured Latinas doesn't work because they are the only Latinxs to be seen in their respective televisual story worlds. Because they embody an entire ethnic demographic, they are suddenly replete with as many Latinx signifiers that mark them as Latinx. These characters cannot be unambiguously Latinx—someone like Cameron Diaz.

Diaz fits the white American phenotype, so if she were in a show that needed a Latina, she actually would not be a viable choice. In other words, she would pass unseen as Latina by all but the most clued in viewers. For Latinxs to be seen on our TVs and on our movie screens, they must carry enough markers of Latinidad. So showrunners and studios and writers ensure that Latinx characters cannot be missed. Add to that the highlighting of stereotypical connotations of Latinxs for the benefit of humor, and it's easy to see what is happening in the examples we mention and the many more we did not.

Latinx Bumbling Buffoons

Lou Adler's *Up in Smoke* (1978) starred Cheech Marin, as Pedro de Pacas, in his first film. He and Tommy Chong passed on the opportunity to star in *Chico and the Man* to focus on making films; in fact, one of Cheech and Chong's comedic routines was the basis for *Chico and the Man*. *Up in Smoke* was a riot.

Many of us Latinxs saw *Up in Smoke* with family and friends. All of us seemed to know someone like Pedro de Pacas, which made it all the more hilarious and meaningful. Cheech's performance may have been one of the first portrayals of a Latinx in film that seemed to be plucked right from the community. The way he spoke, his sense of humor, all of it resonated strongly with Latinx filmgoers. In many

Anthony Stoner (played by Tommy Chong) and Pedro de Pacas (played by Cheech Marin) in *Up in Smoke* (1978)

ways, he was our U.S. Latinx Tin-Tan—*un sujeto transfronterizo*, as Carlos Monsiváis once identified the Mexican comic actor. (The film even created a neologism, the verb to be "cheeched," or to be totally stoned.) Cheech is the Latinx bumbling buffoon, but the jokes are clearly for us, Latinx filmgoers.

In many ways, Pedro (Efren Ramirez) in Jared Hess's *Napoleon Dynamite* (2004) is our twenty-first-century Cheech. Pedro's so lackadaisical, he barely moves his limbs when he walks or lips when he talks. Yet in the end it's Pedro who gets the vote at this all-white high school in Preston, Idaho. (The Latinx demographic in Preston, Idaho, and Northern Utah is more significant than one might think.) Pedro has definitive markings of Latinidad—his thick Spanish accent, his cowboy boots and western dress, his devotion to Catholicism, his lowrider cousins, and so on. But looking a little closer at Pedro reveals him to be the antistereotype in other ways. He's not a criminal, a gangbanger, a drug dealer, or a Latin lover. He's antithetical to the frenzied, hyper, fast-talking comedic relief Latinxs who often appear on TV and in film, like John Leguizamo or Michael Peña. Moreover, Pedro is sensitive, helpful, empathetic, and clever. He's far from the passionate Latinx to which we've become inured. And he becomes class president of the majority white school (with the help of Napoleon's strange dance at the end). He's a Latinx who takes us away from the stereotypes and lazy thinking we've seen ad nauseam in the rest of TV and film.

With *Nacho Libre* (2006) Jared Hess creates another film where he tends to get his Latinx laughter right. Jack Black plays Ignacio: priest by day and Nacho Libre *luchador* by night.

And Hess casts Hector Jimenez as Latinx sidekick, Esqueleto. While there's brownface going on with Jack Black as a Latinx, it's not the same as we discussed with Douglas Fairbanks as Zorro and the earnest disregard of the fact that a white actor plays a Latinx character; the filmmakers didn't see it as a problem because they couldn't conceive of it in a negative light. But Hess, in 2006, knows full well the implications of brownface and blackface. *Nacho Libre* is upfront about its satirical and ironic nature. If a Latinx had been cast as Nacho, it would reek of the stereotype. But Jack Black, a comedian, makes it a farce and a parody. With a Latinx in that particular role, it loses its ability to play the humor a little rough around the edges.

While *Nacho Libre* has its shortcomings, it is much more intriguing and of value than John Landis's *¡Three Amigos!* Nearly all of *Three Amigos!* is shot on a Hollywood back lot. In meta fashion, the protagonists believe they are in a fake location with "fake" Mexicans, but they are actually in a real location with "dangerous" Mexicans. Ironically, the whole production, even the location, is constructed.

Nacho (played by Jack Black) in *Nacho Libre* (2006)

On Matters of Race and Humor

Does it matter *who* is telling the Latinx joke? Jay Leno, as with other late-night talk show comedians, typically began his shows with a comedic monologue that spoke to current events that had occurred within the previous twenty-four hours. Some of his openers included "Forty percent of Mexicans say they would move to the U.S. if they had the chance. The other 60 percent are already here," or "At a speech in San Diego this morning, President Bush said that proposals for massive deportation of illegal immigrants are unrealistic. 'Unrealistic,' he says. Funny, isn't that what Mexico has already done?" and, "It's terrible! Gas now costs $3.85 a gallon. You know, it's cheaper to have illegal immigrants push your car than to fill the tank." As offensive as these jokes are, they are part of a long tradition of fusing ethnic humor with the political. It's not that Latinxs should be off limits. It's that we have so few instances when jokes are written for us to laugh at. When we are the butt of punch lines like these, we're shocked more than amused. If a Latinx comedian like George Lopez used these, he'd likely draw a sense of relief and laughter from us. And Lopez does have many jokes in his routine that have this same sort of thread concerning Latinxs as walking stereotypes. The difference is that he's Latinx and Leno is not. Until we live in a postrace society, maybe the Leno's of the world should stay away from this material.

Why were shows like *Friends* or *Seinfeld* so popular among non-Latinx audiences? They didn't do well among Latinx and African American audiences. Humor is culturally based. Not all jokes translate well. Each of us codifies humor in different ways depending on cultural *and* sociohistorical norms and codes. Indeed, as Christopher discusses elsewhere, what is permissible is also cultural. Think of the occasional memes about how Latina meteorologists in Latin American countries are overwhelmingly sexualized and wear the most revealing clothing. The same holds true for ESPN-type sports broadcasts in Latin American countries. Highly sexualized women aren't even allowed to participate in the substantive sports discussion. They are often there as an outro or intro to a break, and they literally dance in place. There are different standards for what cultures and even demographics within a nation find funny.

The famous Soup Nazi in *Seinfeld* gets a lot of attention. He is the belligerent chef whose soups are impeccable, but he cannot abide anyone who dares to challenge his way of doing things. When someone would cross him, he would shout, "No soup for you!" and would not serve that particular customer. The Soup Nazi was clearly marked as ethnic, but it was hard to discern what that ethnicity was. So, rather than become a stereotype of a particular ethnic group, he became the symbol for the intolerant foodie purist. *Seinfeld* captured this sort of archetypal character that we all knew. So *Seinfeld* works for some and not others, just as *Friends* works for some and not others.

When we laugh when we hear Freddie Prinze, John Leguizamo, Cristela Alonzo, Gabriel Iglesias, or George Lopez do their stand-up routines, we are getting the cultural context for the jokes *and* we react to the way they use body and language to deliver the joke. We might go so far as to say that Latinxs have an identifiably different sense of humor than other groups. Indeed, all distinct cultures must surely have variations on what they find humorous and worthy of laughter. Otherwise, someone somewhere would have come up with the best joke ever, and it would translate perfectly in all languages. This universal best joke, however, would be the end of the game, wouldn't it? It's not essentialist to say Latinxs have a different sense of humor so long as we admit that *all* groups have slight differences in what they consider funny. We Latinxs tend to find George Lopez and Carlos Mencia and Gabriel Iglesias funny (more than non-Latinxs) because they base their comedic routines on their experiences in Latinx culture.

We see with John Leguizamo (many of us think he's a Boricua, but he's of Ecuadorian extraction) how his quick-witted, street-smart, urban-Latinx humor makes it likely that he could only be funny as a Latinx comedian. He plays to audience expectations of the Caribbean, motormouthed Latinx. His one-man shows work singularly within this particular formulation. But he also uses this to make some bold moves. For instance, in his *Spic-O-Rama* show he airs our dirty laundry and pokes fun at our own hang-ups as a Latinx community. And, in his more recent Broadway show *Latin History for Morons*, he uses comedy and satire to educate audiences, Latinxs included, about our untold history.

We see the same use of comedy to wake audiences to real social and political issues with Adam de la Péña's cartoon *Minoriteam* (aired on the Cartoon Network's Adultswim), which features a portly,

John Leguizamo in *Latin History for Morons* (2016)

mustachioed Latino, El Jefe, fighting crime with the world's most powerful leaf blower.

Latinxs who are comedians by trade often fall into the trap of dipping into the most obvious traits of our culture and then laughing at them. Such humor always paints with a broad brush. It's the Stepin Fetchit racialized character routine. It's the boogeyman hiding in the recesses we can't see, just ready to jump out at a moment's notice. For Latinxs who are inextricably linked with their culture, highlighting these little bits for their humor isn't as potentially insulting because we know it doesn't embody the totality of the community.

Latinx rapper and humorist Lil' Mono has a rap on social media about *pan dulce*—the various sweet breads and confectionaries we see in many Latinx communities. His video shows him pedaling around the neighborhood on a large tricycle selling his bread. It's funny because it does reflect the Latinx community, but importantly it's only a tiny bit of our culture. Those unfamiliar with Latinx culture would probably only laugh *at* the video, and not *with* it. It's difficult to create humor based on one's own minority culture without playing dangerously close to stereotypes and caricatures.

Brown versus Light Latinx Humor

There was a moment when *The George Lopez Show* was canceled. At that same time, Louis C.K. was becoming an unstoppable comedic star. Lopez is mestizo, Louis is light skinned (Mexican and U.S. Irish

Catholic). Was the TV industry telling us that George Lopez and the Latinxs in his show didn't have the right "look" for general U.S. audiences? Lopez, the prototypical mestizo brown guy, is the sort of Brown Buffalo that Oscar Zeta Acosta imagined himself to be—larger than life, bombastic, in your face, and unapologetic. Or was there something about Louis C.K.'s jokes that made him more relatable—more bankable? How many white American households, even today, can relate to Latinx culture in its comedic form? The kind of humor that Lopez creates is, if deployed by a non-Latinx, highly stereotypical. In an age of heightened sensitivity to diversity and awareness of stereotypes, some white audiences might not want to laugh at such ethnicity-based humor.

Comedy is all about relatability. That's why so many comedians start a joke with a situation that many in the audience will be familiar with even if it's within the context of the comedian's own life. In the case of Louis C.K., his jokes about divorce (over half of Americans are affected by it), sex, and depression resonate with most of the U.S. demographic.

That Louis C.K. has fallen from grace with the #MeToo revelations should be mentioned. Suddenly his relatable jokes about sex and dysfunction fall flat. With the revelations of his predatory ways and sexual assaults, audiences no longer see a divide between his comedy and the biographical fact of his unconscionable treatment of women.

Latinxs Behind and In Front of the Camera Matter

CW's *Jane the Virgin*, ABC's *Cristela* (canceled), and Netflix's *One Day at a Time* (canceled) have us laughing with Latinxs and our raison d'être—from squeaking by as Catholics to our macho and machista rituals and love of telenovela dramas. Latinxs are integral to the storytelling process—from writing to portrayal.

When Latinxs have a substantive role in the creation of Latinx stories or stories with Latinxs, we get a much better quality of product. *Jane the Virgin* and *Ugly Betty* are shows originally created in Latin America. *Cristela* is based on the comedy of Cristela Alonzo. And Netflix put an all-Latinx cast in front of the camera in the reboots of *One Day at a Time*.

When we have a Latinx presence behind and in front of the cameras, we can go to interesting places in our comedy. Take the episode in *Jane the Virgin* when the nuns at the school where Jane teaches start to hand out Jane medallions. They want to drum up business, so they're promoting Jane as a saint who can bring the miracle of conception to barren couples. And *Jane the Virgin* places center stage an issue the church has had to deal with of late: same sex couplings. The show builds into its telenovela story world love affairs between women: Dr. Luisa Alver and her stepmother, Rose, followed by her falling in love with Susana, *and* a passionate romance between Petra and her lawyer, Jane Ramos (played by Rosario Dawson). It's funny, and it's a biting commentary on the desperate moves of Catholicism and the church to survive in the twenty-first century and within the traditionally religious Latinx community. Indeed, *Jane the Virgin* smartly draws on the issue of how organized religion in the United States is losing members every year and how the rapidly declining numbers of younger members is causing widespread panic across the board—from Catholics to Southern Baptists to Latter-day Saints. It also engages

Jane Medallions in *Jane the Virgin* (season 1, episode 7, 2014)

with issues concerning the Catholic Church, which is such a significant part of many Latinx communities. And it does so, dare we say, in an authentic way. It doesn't seem like the product of some writer who says, "Here's an idea! Latinxs tend to be Catholic. Let's do something with . . . the Virgin Mary!" The show is much more nuanced and sensitive than that, which is why it succeeds to such a large degree.

When Latinx comedies are made well, there is money to be made. The runaway success of Mexican comedic star Eugenio Derbez's *Instructions Not Included* (*No se aceptan devoluciones*, 2013) is due to the fact that it's funny and that it raises some serious issues, such as the dangers of border crossing, the very real role children play in translating for monolingual Spanish-speaking parents, and even the tragic passing of the daughter Maggie (Loreta Peralta) at the film's close. However, Eugenio Derbez as the protagonist, Valentín Bravo, is permanently fixed within the oversexed and bumbling buffoon stereotype. Importantly, too, the film eschewed the drug-lord, queen-of-the-south, prison experience that has come to represent so much of Latinidad on the screen.

Instructions Not Included was a wake-up call for Hollywood moguls: Latinxs do spend money going to the movies. The film broke box-office records on both sides of the U.S.-Mexico border. Should we be surprised that it was a film that gravitates toward Latinx comic buffoonery that packed the house? Not only that, but Derbez's film is in Spanish. And it made huge money. Studio executives may have been left wondering whether it was a fluke or whether it was an indication of something more. A film about Latinxs—speaking in Spanish—could do well in the United States. *Coco* was an even bigger smash, and it code-switches quite regularly between English and Spanish.

Yes. Latinxs go to the movies in great numbers, but we don't want to lead our readers into a trap of thinking that Latinxs *only* watch films with Latinxs in them or that are about issues relevant to the Latinx community. Remember our discussion earlier in the book concerning going to see *Cesar Chavez* or the blockbuster *Noah*. We agree that many Latinxs went to see *Noah*.

The Curious Case of Brown Minstrelsy and Wrap-Up

The history of brown minstrelsy includes our presence as somehow intrinsically good at dancing. We're fine with this kind of stereotype.

On the silver screen, we'd already seen the so-called rumbles transmogrify into dance and song numbers in *West Side Story* (1961). Latinxs were battling Anglos, and not with knives and guns but in dance. It gets crazy between the Jets and the Sharks when Latina Maria (Natalie Wood in brownface) dares to cross the ethnoracial tracks to be with her Anglo love interest, Tony, a former Jet. It's the dance that becomes the release valve for the building threat of brown sullying white in this romance that threatens miscegenation.

Latinxs have no special gene that generates an amazing dance ability. Not all Latinxs can dance. That may come as a shock to some, since Latinx culture is steeped in certain identifiable expressions—music, food, and dance, for example. When representations of Latinidad on the screen concentrate on dancing, on music, and on food, then audiences are led to think that *all* Latinos must be great dancers or musicians or cooks. Oscar Hijuelos, the first Latinx author to win a Pulitzer Prize for Literature, had all of that in his novel *The Mambo Kings Play Songs of Love*. It's all in the title. Machismo, patriarchy, music, love, passion. His novel is excellent, but consider what Junot Díaz, the only other Latinx to win the Pulitzer Prize for Literature, does in his award-winning novel *The Brief Wondrous Life of Oscar Wao*. His title character is the most non-Latinx Latinx we've ever seen. He's dark-skinned because of his African ancestry via the Dominican Republic. He's passionate about nerd culture. He reads and writes with reckless abandon. And he fears he will die a virgin. The novel creates a Latinx protagonist unlike any we have ever seen in the United States, ever. There is no Latinx character like Oscar Wao before him. After him, we see a similar, yet less tragic, figure in Manny Delgado (played by Rico Rodriguez) in the ABC hit show *Modern Family*.

This isn't to say that Latinx culture doesn't revere dancing and music. It does. But the *ab ovo* "we are born to dance" sentiment makes us pause. That kind of thinking can easily be reverse engineered to express notions that "all Latinxs can dance," or worse. That's not to say we Latinxs don't value dancing or don't want to be great dancers, of course.

Hollywood loves to pull Latinxs back into our bodies—as needing our siestas (the D. W. Griffith legacy) or as using our bodies to violently destroy other bodies (the drug dealer, gangbanger, or Latin-lover legacy). Hollywood does something a bit different with Latinas. The

Eva Rodriguez (played by Zoe Saldana) in *Center Stage* (2000)

gravitational pull is toward the slinking, glistening, brown-skinned, dancing body. Think of the role that put Zoe Saldana on the map as ballerina Eva Rodríguez in *Center Stage* (2000).

Think, too, of the way Jessica Alba went from badass metahuman Alex in *Dark Angel* to Honey Daniels in *Honey* (2003), where it's her dancing body that pulls her out of the ghetto. Latinas in particular must have a certain look, a certain body: dark hair, dark eyes, olive/tanned skin, large hips, thin waists. This physicality is just another in the long list of Latinx signifiers that announce that the bodies audiences are staring at are Latina bodies.

Shakira uses her body—her hips and pole-dancing routines—as a vehicle for her voice and lyrics. She sells albums. The video for "Hips Don't Lie" is almost entirely made up of Shakira, her hips and lots of skin exposed, gyrating to the rhythm of the song. It was quite popular, and it remains so on YouTube, having been watched over half a billion times. Let's also consider what Wyclef Jean says in the song: "I never really knew that she could dance like this / She makes a man wants to speak Spanish!" But the Latina body can also threaten non-Latinx audiences. Think of Jennifer Lopez's music video "Booty," with Iggy Azalea, where their strategic rubbing of brown booty against white booty aims to repel white Puritan America. The video starts with a literal "warning," and then it is an onslaught of large derrieres belonging to the aforementioned women.

We've seen other instances in which the brown body threatens and gets a whitewashed makeover. This happened with appropriations of Latinx and African American beats and moves by Elvis and Buddy Holly. Interestingly, Holly married a Puerto Rican named Maria Elena Santiago, and she has been a steadfast defender of Holly's legacy. Unlike many other white singers and songwriters who were strongly influenced by black music, Holly was shaped by white singers like Hank Williams, Hank Snow, and Bob Wills, and by the black artists who were surging ahead with rhythm and blues (R and B). Holly's true innovation was bringing these two musical worlds together. He would go on to influence Elvis and the Beatles, among countless others.

It happened with Irish Johnny Castle (Patrick Swayze) in *Dirty Dancing* (1987), with his made-safe hip thrusts and grinds as he wins over "Baby" (Jennifer Grey). Swayze's mambo moves brought a return of over $200 million for the film. We don't want to slip into an essentialist logic here. Of course, we recognize that mambo is a dance *style* and thus belongs to anyone who can do it. What's problematic is that yet again it's a white guy who is represented doing this when it might've been a brown guy.

In the sequel to *Dirty Dancing*, director Guy Ferland made the mambo moves safe by moving the narrative to a far-off land and distant time: Cuba just before the Revolution. *Dirty Dancing: Havana Nights* (2004) doesn't hold back in its use of Latinx stereotypes as all bodily, hypersexualized Others (in this case, Diego Luna as Javier Suarez) whose sole raison d'être is to seduce unsuspecting, innocent white female tourists.

Dirty Dancing: Havana Nights tries desperately to announce its connection to Latinx culture, but it is yet another example of lazy storytelling. It tries to capitalize, literally, on the exotic Latinx trope—from its setting, its stereotypical characters, and the music. But, despite the efforts of Diego Luna, it is a pretty abysmal film, currently with a score of 22 percent on Rotten Tomatoes. But here we have the kind of Latinidad and Latinx dance culture that comes together, *and it does not work.*

Whether it's mambo or salsa, the Latinx or Latina seducer-dancer appears over and over again in dance flicks. In *Dance with Me* (1998), Puerto Rican singer Chayanne as Rafael Infante salsas his way into Vanessa Williams's heart. In *Shall We Dance* (2004), Jennifer Lopez as dance instructor Paulina dances to tunes like "Santa Maria del Buen Ayre" and fires up an otherwise taciturn, staid, lonely, middle-aged John Clark (Richard Gere). Lambada is known as "the forbidden dance," and so, naturally, Joe Silberg's *Lambada* (1990) features Latinx break-dancer Adolfo "Shabba-Doo" Quiñones as Ramone, who uses his dance moves to persuade Latinxs in East L.A. to hit the books. What unites these dance flicks and others is the idea of passion run amok, the idea of Latinx culture, and the idea of body movement as expressive and irresistible. In all of these films the seductive powers are raised to the third power: Latinx culture, Latinx dance, Latinx body. Who can resist that?

Chapter 4

PIXELATED AND REEL LATINX
NIÑOS, TEENS, AND MORE

Formative Sights and Sounds

Before many of us Latinxs could walk, all variety of Mexican sights and sounds were in our lives. Even though one of us was in Mexico City (Frederick) and the other (Christopher) in the Texas panhandle, *El Chavo del Ocho* and *El Chapulín Colorado* streamed into our *salas*. Talk about a perfect superhero for us Latinx crumb snatchers!

The super-high energy, supervillain-vanquishing Chesperito (Roberto Gomez Bolaños) could shrink in size and use his bike horn to paralyze villains and his Chipote Chillón to smash foes—all while never feeling the need to change out of his pajamas. Children's programming on Spanish TV networks such as Galavision, Univision, and Telemundo helped shape the translingual imaginary of many Latinxs. With nothing that spoke to Latinx culture in a meaningful way on American network TV, Latinxs turned to shows such as the ones Gomez Bolaños created.

Television programs in the United States didn't catch wind of this need for a multilingual, polycultural experience for *niños* for decades to come. That wouldn't be until the year 2000, when Nickelodeon launched *Dora the Explorer*, introducing the Latina animated character Dora to all variety of ethnoracial and linguistic audiences.

With her success came other spin-offs, such as her cousin's show, *Go, Diego, Go!* (2005–2006), Disney's *Handy*

Dora and Boots in *Dora the Explorer* (season 4, episode 404, 2016)

Manny (2006–2013), and *Dora and Friends* (2013–). Kids around the country were learning their ABCs, puzzle-solving strategies, and some Spanglishisms. Setting aside its construction of yet another Latinx *bandido* figure (Swiper), if we strip the shows down, we see in each—and *Handy Manny* takes it to the extreme—a kind of Spanish taught that completely disconnects from cultural reference. It's a Spanish that's supposed to be functional, like Manny's wrench used to change a tire, or *llanta*. It's an erasure of the full range of Latinx culture. And in its place is the cementing in children's minds the idea that Latinxs are only useful as tools, arms, legs—braceros who work to sustain the Haves.

Fortunately, we also had Jorge Gutiérrez's far more creative show *El Tigre* (also Nickelodeon 2007–2008). While it only had a short run, it showed the world just how innovative programming could be for *niños* across the country. Gutiérrez's flash animation does more than dazzle kids. It gives kinetic force to stories that deeply affirm Latinx culture.

It appealed to young and older kids (tweens and teens), and it actually had an overarching narrative. And, remarkably, it was set in "Miracle City," which was a stand-in for Mexico City. Here and also in his feature animated film *The Book of Life*, Jorge Gutiérrez not only avoids blatant stereotypes, but he also creates everyday superhero types Latinxs can relate to and affirm.

Without reason, Nickelodeon canceled *El Tigre*—even though it generated ratings similar to those for the megahit *SpongeBob Square-Pants* at the same stage of development. Unusual, since new TV shows are renewed if they receive high ratings. This is yet another case of non-Latinx network executives' gatekeeping good Latinx TV. They

Manny Rivera in *El Tigre* (season 1, episode 6, 2007)

probably canceled it because they didn't understand the cultural references; they weren't its *ideal audience.*

Fortunately, this wasn't the last we'd see of Jorge Gutiérrez's Latinx animations. With financing from Academy Award–winning Mexican director Guillermo del Toro, Gutiérrez created *The Book of Life* (2014)—a story that makes clear that its ideal audience is Latinx but that covers other marginalized subjects. La Muerte delivers the story exclusively to the detention kids: the Goth-Latinx Luka Ramirez, Indian American Sanjay, Asian American Jane, and Russian American Sasha. The story is for them and for audiences packing our theaters who also feel as if they've been pushed aside by society. It's the first feature-length animated film that's made first for *Othered* kids and teens, then *Othered adults* (let's not forget Ice Cube voicing the Candle Maker), *then* the mainstream.

Animated Brownfaces

Unlike *The Book of Life*, which featured Latinxs Zoe Saldana, Danny Trejo, Cheech Marin, Eugenio Derbez, Diego Luna, and Ana de la Reguera (Mexican), among others, there's a long tradition of mainstream animation that casts non-Latinx voice actors to play Latinx characters. And, as Dora has grown from preschooler to tween, so too have her tone, rhythm, and pitch shifted from being voiced by Kathleen Herles to Caitlin Sanchez *and* Fátima Ptacek. While the creators did cast a Latina to voice her as a teen, overwhelmingly she's been voiced by non-Latinxs.

Mel Blanc voicing Speedy Gonzales was the beginning of this deep, long trend of non-Latinx voice actors playing animated Latinx characters, as we noted in the previous chapter. We see the same with other underrepresented groups, such as African Americans, or of an "ethnic" actor to play an "ethnic" part, as with casting Cheech Marin as Banzai in *The Lion King* (1994). In his performance, he is ambiguously ethnic, as is Whoopi Goldberg, who voiced the other hyena. They play the characters without overt markers of racialized performance, though Marin's hyena at one point says to Scar, "I said . . . que pasa?" And John Leguizamo voices the comic buffoon Sid the Sloth in *Ice Age* (2005). While we think these performances are valuable, especially when we are talking about animals or inanimate objects that in an ideal world wouldn't have markers of Latinidad, we're not quite there yet.

The casting of Robin Williams as Ramon in *Happy Feet 2* is a case in point. We don't mean to say that Williams or any other voice actor can *only* do impressions within their own identity or racial community. However, in the deeply imbalanced world of representation that traditionally sidelines Latinx voice actors generally, the casting of non-Latinx in brown-voice, so to speak, remains problematic. And, hypothetically and idealistically speaking, even if we lived in a reel world where representations all stood on equal footing, we'd still demand that a non-Latinx voice actor like Williams perform (e.g., tone, rhythm, intonation, pitch) in ways that didn't slip into a Latin-lover stereotype (or any other). For Latinx voice performers, this is common sense.

Cheech Marin's voicing of Alonzo Julio Frederico de Tito in Disney's *Oliver and Company* (1988) marked an important moment. It was the first time a Latinx actually voiced a Latinx in mainstream animated film.

It would take decades before we began to see a more systematic bucking of the brown-voice trend in Hollywood. When Diego Luna voices Manolo Sánchez or Zoe Saldana plays María Posada in *The Book of Life*, they don't voice fixed stereotypes such as the Latin lover or hypersexual Latina. In *Cloudy with a Chance of Meatballs*, Benjamin Bratt's English/Spanish code-switching, complex voice performance of Manny creates tension with the script's stereotyping of him as a jack-of-all-trades. And Michael Peña breathes some complexity into the chunky, baseball-cap-wearing Latinx taco truck owner Tito in *Turbo* (2013); Luis Guzman's Nuyorican voicing of the brother, Angelo, adds another oral/aural layer of Latinoness to the animated film. Their Latinidad is allowed (or encouraged) to come through in these layered ways.

This said, not all Latinxs voice against stereotype—or in ways that complicate Latinx identities. This seems to be especially the case with Latinas. Sofía Vergara's voicing of Carmen in *Happy Feet 2*, with a thick Spanish accent and with nuances and intonations, drips with the exotic and hypersexual. Penélope Cruz's voicing of a thick-accented, exotic Special Agent Juarez (*G-Force*) is also tagged with a Flamenco-styled sound leitmotif.

Mainstreamed Latinxs Matter
Only as Sidekicks and Laboring Bodies

While today's creators are getting part of it right by casting actual Latinxs to voice Latinx characters, the writing of the characters remains limited to the corporeal as ingesting, laboring, cleaning, or fixing characters. Cheech Marin went from voicing a cat and, later, a hyena, to the '59 Impala lowrider Ramone (and his license plate L0WNSL0) in *Cars* (2006), *Cars 2* (2011), and *Cars 3* (2017). Cristela Alonzo, who had her own short-lived ABC sitcom *Cristela*, appears as Cruz Ramirez, the yellow sports coupe that trains Lightning McQueen (voiced by Owen Wilson) in *Cars 3*. Ramone plays the sidekick in the original film to McQueen, who wins the day.

The character Manny in *Cloudy with a Chance of Meatballs 2* exists in a story that's all about food—and its dangers. When Manny sees a marauding monster approach, he announces "TACO-dile Supreme" with great delight and with an accompaniment of mariachi. Manny and others who make up a multiethnic team end up doing all the work (and cleanup) while the entrepreneurial white protagonist, Flint Lockwood, ends up the one celebrated at the end for saving the day.

The Tacodile in *Cloudy with a Chance of Meatballs 2* (2009)

In *Turbo* the creators write Tito as always listening to hip-hop, and they write the Latina, Paz (Michelle Rodriguez), as a mechanic—and draw her with a rather large derriere that the DreamWorks's camera lens likes to hover over. It's the Latinxs who help the white guy (snail), Turbo (voiced by Ryan Reynolds), win the race—and save the day.

Paz (played by Michelle Rodriguez) in *Turbo* (2013)

Mainstreaming animated Latinxs as primarily associated with the body would not be so off putting if creators were writing Latinx characters in a wide variety of roles. We don't want to put more straightjackets on Latinidad, either. It's okay that Cheech (and Goldberg, for that matter) play the hyenas in *The Lion King*. The characters are dastardly and funny—and *should* be played by voice actors with comedic chops. And it's okay that Cheech's Benzai doesn't *sound* Latinx, deflecting Latinx pop cultural sleuths like ourselves from criticizing the animalizing of a Latinx character. Cheech voices a hyena, after all.

We don't want to take a position where we say Latinxs must always play the moral, ethical, handsome, and heroic characters. However, we Latinx critics won't be satisfied till Hollywood does more than just voicecast and/or create us as villains, buffoons, erotic exotica (animal or otherwise), or as handy street hip-hopsters.

Whitewashing Latinxs

The Simpsons is certainly one of the wittiest shows on TV—and the longest-running comedy in TV history (twenty-nine seasons and counting). It's hugely popular among Latinx viewers. Oddly, however, the show doesn't feature any continuously present Latinx characters. In one episode, Krusty the Klown takes Bart and Lisa to "The Happiest Place on Earth": Tijuana. The episode ends with a faux montage of Bart, Lisa, and other Springfield kids wearing sombreros and getting wasted. Homer occasionally boogies to an identifiable Latinx mambo or salsa tune.

In "Who Shot Mr. Burns?" Tito Puente makes an appearance as substitute music teacher at Springfield Elementary and a suspect in the shooting of Mr. Burns. He composes the song "Señor Burns": "It may not surprise you / But all of us despise you / Please die, and fry, in Hell / You rotten rich old wretch. / Adios Viejo!" There's the episode "Special Edna" that features the character Julio Estudiante working with inner-city youth. In typical *Simpsons* fashion, it's a parodic palimpsest of Olmos as Jaime Escalante in the biopic *Stand and Deliver* (1988).

Tito Puente (played by Tito Puente) in *The Simpsons* (season 6, episode 25, 1995)

And there's the appearance of Bumblebee Man, the star of Spanish-language TV network Ocho. The Mexican allusions (a luchador and Chapulín Colorado mash-up) that inform Bumblebee Man's characterization appeal to a Latinx audience. However, his clipped, hyper-exaggerated Spanish accent and later confession that he's Belgian undo all this.

The Simpsons mainstreams (whitewashes) Latinidad by sidestepping altogether Latinx voice performers; it does the same with Asian American and African American performers, too. Spanish Jewish American Hank Azaria voices most of the Spanish characters, including Bumblebee Man and Señor Spielbergo, the poor man's Mexican version of Steven Spielberg hired to make a film of Mr. Burns for the Springfield Film Festival. Burns to Spielbergo: "I want you to do for me what Spielberg did for Oskar Schindler." Spielbergo to Burns, a bit nonplussed: "But Señor Schindler es bueno. Señor Burns . . . es . . . el diablo." Hank Azaria voices Asian American Apu. Notably, the show and Azaria have been the subject of sustained criticism that reached a crescendo with the release of the documentary *The Problem with*

Apu. Azaria has since publicly stated that he is willing to step aside from playing Apu.

We see this same whitewashing in nonanimation films an TV. We think of Disney's tradition of casting light-skinned Latinxs as ambiguously marked Latinxs. We mentioned already Jenna Ortega as Harley Diaz in *Stuck in the Middle* as well as Demi Lovato and Selena Gomez; the latter two began this career trend as *niñas* in *Barney and Friends* (2002–2004).

We also mentioned how Disney casts Selena Gomez as Alex in *Wizards of Waverly Place* (2007) and identifies her as Latina through her mom, Theresa, played by Cuban Latina María Canals Barrera, and through food: the family runs a restaurant. Mainstream Latinidad is consumable with just enough Latinx passing and Latinx food, and here they are owners of the restaurant and not workers, so the creators probably thought this would also be a way to appeal to the American-dreamer (capitalist) ideal audience. It's a televisual version of folks who like to go eat at their local Mexican restaurant but who disdain the *actual* presence of Latinxs in the United States.

We take pause to speculate. Might the thought process for the creators of a show such as *Wizards* or *Camp Rock* or fill in the blank have gone something like "we can't create a family of mechanics (too stereotypical) or teachers (done already with *Girl Meets World*), so let's go for a restaurant"? Audiences in the United States will believe this; it is one aspect of reality that is real and can be reconstructed. The result falls short because Disney tends to have blinders on when it comes to *seeing* Latinxs in all walks of life. Disney often goes for the safe and readily digestible: Latinx characters created as cooks (kitchens/food generally) *and* as passing (light skinned).

Latinx Passing and Inhabiting Whiteness

While the phenotypically brown Gabriela Rodriguez (Cuban American actress) plays Brooke Nichols, there's no Latinness to speak of when Lovato plays the character Charlotte Adams in the Disney Channel show *As the Bell Rings*. We see a pattern of whitening in the casting of Lovato as the princess, Rosalinda Montoya, in *Princess Protection Program* (2009), where Latinidad can be marked because Montoya is an aristocrat from a land far away (a fictionalized Costa

Luna) versus Selena Gomez, cast as the down-home, rural character Carter Mason, who is passing as white.

It's okay to be marked Latinx if it's at a safe, exotic distance (accent or geographic location); otherwise, Disney's Latinxs have to pass as nonthreatening, whitewashed characters or as chubby, funny kids such as Jorge in *Bunk'd*— a show about a summer camp where Latinx actor Nathan Arenas plays Jorge, a portly, smart, *and* devious character. One way or another, Disney stereotypes (Jorge) or whitewashes by casting Latinas who pass to play such roles as Carter Mason, Brooke Nichols, and Charlotte Adams.

(Notably, Jessica Alba's career has been built in her being cast in ethnoracially ambiguous roles. She wasn't a Latina in *Dark Angel*. She is an example of how many Latinas on screen can play up their Latinidad or downplay it

Rosalinda Montoya (played by Demi Lovato) in *Princess Protection Program* (2009)

to the point that they are essentially Anglo characters.)

We would like to complicate this scenario somewhat by asking if perhaps we should consider passing as more of a strategic inhabiting of whiteness. Within a reel history that has typecast Latinx as only X, Y, or Z in contrast with white actors allowed to play *all* ethnic and identities or subjectivities, perhaps it's okay that a Lovato or Gomez is cast as a Carter or a Brooke or a Charlotte. Furthermore, as we've mentioned earlier with the diversity of morphology and phenotype that we as authors of this book represent, Latinidad in the United States is multifaceted and multivalent. Not all Latinxs look and sound like Cheech Marin in *Born in East L.A.* Some look and sound like

Brooke Nichols and Charlotte Adams—the ambiguously ethnic characters. While there is, in fact, cultural plentitude of expression in actuality, the narrative plentitude (per Nguyen) reveals the disparity in representation.

The Principle of Ubiquitous Whiteness

Elsewhere, Christopher uses the "principle of ubiquitous whiteness" as a concept to identify how, unless a film or TV show explicitly identifies a character's Latinidad, audiences generally assume that that character is white even if their eyes tell them they are seeing a Latinx actor.

In other words, when Demi Lovato or Jessica Alba play clearly identifiable Latinas, suddenly all of this other baggage is thrown into the mix. However, if an Alba or a Lovato play an ambiguously ethnic or white character, they are passing and hiding something; their Latinidad is under erasure. Isabel Molina-Guzmán usefully contrasts "color-blind" TV programming (ambiguously ethnic or white) with "color-conscious" TV programing, which develops "characters with ethnic and racial

Max Guevara aka "X5–452" (played by Jessica Alba) in *Dark Angel* (season 1, episode 1, 2000)

cultural and experiential specificity and thereby more complexity" (*Latinas and Latinos on TV*, 9).

So, we ask, What is acceptable? What works? Is it possible for Latinxs to be represented properly on screen? If we begin to have Latinxs in higher numbers on the screen, so long as there is all manner of Latinx characters played by a range of Latinxs, we'll be less worried about whether they are saints (or sinners) inhabiting whiteness or blackness or alienness. While we want to complicate categories of what qualifies as good Latinx representation and bad, we also know that reel representations of Latinxs operate within an entire system of reconstructing race, gender, and sexuality that continues to be lopsided and simplistic. Whites don't worry about this because there are *so many white characters*. They have narrative plentitude. Put simply, we haven't seen the *Coco* moment permeate reel film and televisual storytelling, and so as critics we're forced to call out the good and the bad.

Mainstreamed Latinx LGBTQ

Whitewashing or passing aside, there's the issue of other important ways that Latinxs exist as intersectional subjects, including sexuality. In 2010, queer Latinx creator Silvio Horta of *Ugly Betty* has Justin Suarez (played by Italian Puerto Rican American actor Mark Indelicto) come out of the closet; this and his intimate moment with his boyfriend broke ground on prime time not just because of the racial representation but because it was the first time a teen character had come out on TV. With *Glee*, the show cast Naya Rivera as lipstick lesbian teen Santana. In contrast with Justin, Ryan Murphy and the other cocreators marked her Latinidad by name, Santana, and not family and cultural traditions.

These representations of queer Latinxs were far more interesting and complex than some earlier ones, such as Oscar Nuñez in *The Office*, who is the constant butt end of queer-bashing jokes. On one occasion, his boss, Michael (Steve Carell), tells Oscar that he's going to have a colonoscopy and asks, "In your experience, what should I be expecting, in terms of sensation. Or, emotions. . . . Is there anything I can do to make it more pleasurable for me or for Dr. Shandri? My main concern is should I have a safe word?" And then there's that moment when Michael asks Oscar, "Is there a term besides Mexican that you prefer? Something less offensive?"

Today prime time continues to write LGBTQ Latinxs into shows. We think readily of *Supergirl* (2015–) and of Latina lesbian Detective Margarita "Maggie" Sawyer (played by Anglo Floriana Lima)—and this at a moment when the show went from the prime-time spotlight on CBS to CW. And we think of the even more fully realized out teen Latinx lesbian Elena Alvarez (played by Isabella Gomez of Colombian ancestry) in Gloria Calderón Kellet's created show for Netflix *One Day at a Time* (2017–2019). Here, not only does the character Elena do a great job at calling attention to the straight privilege in the family, but she also wrestles with her own passing privilege as the member of the family with light skin who speaks English without an accent.

Devon (played by Roberta Colindrez) in *I Love Dick* (season 1, episode 3, 2017)

Even more radically, Amazon Prime's *I Love Dick* (2017) features Mexican-born Argentinian Honduran Latinx lesbian actor Roberta Colindrez (known for her role as Joan in the Broadway adaptation of Alison Bechdel's *Fun Home*), who plays a genderqueer Mexican American. Her character, Devon, is more than a sidebar to the show. She's likely the most powerful queer Latinx subject (actor/role) ever to appear on TV. In one of many powerful scenes she commands her (their) partner to "suck my cock."

While the trajectory has been toward TV programming to create more interesting Latinx characters who occupy several marginalized identity positions, it's still rather scattershot. When we've seen a long history of writers and executives inconsistently creating Latinx characters, it's no surprise that creating intersectional characters will be uneven. So, if we revisit Santana for a moment, we see that while she's comfortably out as lesbian, she has absolutely no Latinidad beyond her name and dark-brown phenotype. But then we see with Justin that his Latinidad becomes *only* his association with cultural tradition and food—both identified as central narrative ingredients for the show and the plot.

Within this schema, there is the hybrid Latina/Klingon B'Elanna Torres, played by Latina actress Roxann Dawson, in *Star Trek: Voyager* (1995–2001). Her surname is Torres, and she is played by a Latina, and yet the seven-year run of the show focused almost entirely on her Klingon heritage and not her Latinx ancestry. In the show, her Latinx ethnicity is occluded by her humanity. Her makeup and Klingon forehead prosthetic literally mask her Latinidad, and she's only ambiguously ethnic when the Klingon part of the character moves aside, which rarely happens. This appears to be another instance of creating an exotic, otherworldly gendered Latinidad that's more readily consumable than one closer to terrestrial home.

Not so incidentally, we can say the same of Marvel's comic-book character America Chavez. She's out lesbian and identifiable Latina through her Spanish/English code-switching, link to her luchador *abuelitas*, and cultural references generally. However, even with a queer Latinx (Gabby Rivera) writing the character, her *mamás*, Amalia and Elena Chavez, raise her in the Utopian Parallel, an out-of-time, otherworldly dimension.

Controlling the Latinx Look

We want to see TV and films that depict Latinas in all shapes and sizes—and not the sexy, "spicy" bombshells and sexually portrayed characters played by Sofía Vergara and Salma Hayek.

So, we at first celebrate the casting of, for instance, Madison De La Garza as Juanita Solis, daughter of Gabi and Carlos Solis, in *Desperate Housewives*. However, we slip into dismay when her Latinidad is anchored in a body that's identified in the show (and the *mamá* Gabi) as overweight—as abnormal. We see the same with Betty Suarez in *Ugly Betty*. Mainstream reel creators imagine Latinas as spicy and slightly exotic on the screen; this is Hollywood and prime-time TV's default setting. When Latinas are created outside of this sexpot characterization, not as gorgeous or fit or some nearly unattainable figure, then there is something wrong with them.

Moreover, there tends to be another discernable pattern. The darker along the phenotypic brown spectrum the characters/actors, the more rotund they seem to be in the reel imaginary. In addition to Juanita Solis and Betty Suarez just mentioned, there's Manny (Rico Rodriguez) in *Modern Family*, Penelope (Justina Machado) in *One Day at a Time*, Alberto (Gabriel Iglesias) in *Cristela*, Jorge (Nathan Arenas) in *Bunk'd*, and many others. In film, we've seen Latinx directors ask their actors to gain weight to *look* more Mexican or Latinx. We think readily of Alejandro González Iñárritu, who forced Adriana Barraza to gain weight to look more like a Mexican maid in *Babel*, and director Anthony Lucero, who did the same with Diana Elizabeth Torres to play the Latina *mamá* Juana in *East Side Sushi* (2016).

Juana (played by Diana Elizabeth Torres) in *East Side Sushi* (2016)

Twenty-first-century TV has created young Latinx characters who push hard against the long history of straightjacketing Latinidad. This includes Manny in *Modern Family*. He is smart, wise, globally cultured—and the ethical compass to his mixed-race family. Jorge in *Bunk'd* is a character cut from a similar mold. In *Bunk'd*, a show about a hijinks-filled summer camp, Jorge is written as both smart and mischievous, with just enough nerdiness to make him endearing. And we can say the same of Elena Alvarez in *One Day at a Time*. She's even smarter and more complex than Manny or Jorge. All of these characters break tired stereotypes. In the case of Manny, he radically disrupts representations of smart Latinxs as only skinny reprobates who are intellectually and morally bankrupt, as per *Stand and Deliver*. Jorge speaks without a trace of Spanish accent, and he is one of the featured members of the cast. Manny, Jorge, and Elena are heavier-set Latinxs who are smart, complex, and ethically interesting. Our communities are filled with smart, funny, endomorphs. Manny and Elena show the world that it's okay to be a smart, funny, brown kid in America.

We all love Robert Rodriguez's *Spy Kids* films as entertaining and fun. The phenotypes of the actors don't announce them as Latinx, but the whole world that Rodriguez composes is somehow infused with a Latinidad. From the jet-pack flying adventures through cities where Latinxs and Spanish simply exist to where Latinxs are both protagonists and antagonists to where uncles are inventors and *mamás* and *papás* are spies, these are films where being Latinx is simply a matter of fact. Rodriguez's *Spy Kids* is a kind of Latinx utopia—a vision of a potential future. They gesture toward a moment when the mainstream *reel* imaginary will represent Latinidad as a matter of fact without any heavy-handed signaling and with respect for cultural tradition and ancestral past. In this sense, Rodriguez presents a postrace utopia but not a Latinx assimilated utopia. *Spy Kids* movies reconstruct a Latinidad where Latinxs can look and sound all sorts of ways, and they can be in just about any role you can imagine. These expressions of Latinidad are both permissible and plentiful in Rodriguez's story worlds. They show audiences what is possible in terms of how Latinxs might be imagined on screen and what might be attainable in our own day-to-day realities.

Latinx as Gangbanger

There's a tradition of reel reconstructions of Latinx teens as gang-bangers in need of saving. While in *Stand and Deliver*, Ramón Menéndez does a great job reconstructing an important moment in our Latinx history (Jaime Escalante and his work with Latinx students at Garfield High), the mainstream copycat films such as *Dangerous Minds* (1995), among others, portray a barrio that needs reforming, and they use a white-savior formula to get the job done. So in *Dangerous Minds*, Michelle Pfeiffer plays a former U.S. Marine, LouAnne Johnson, who *tames* a set of unruly East Palo Alto Latinx gangbangers. And in *Freedom Writers*, Hillary Swank is cast as another fish-out-of-water white woman teacher who saves inner-city kids. The message is that Latinx and kids of color generally are in need of saving. Their parents don't care, their teachers have given up, and the principal humors the idealistic teacher until he or she has had enough and complaints mount. Created as feel-good movies for white audiences—and in the case of *Freedom Writers*, based on actual events—they nevertheless end up powerfully reinforcing the misguided notion that *all* minority students are gang members or dealing drugs or are one step away from incarceration.

Non-Latinx Complex Creations

It *is* possible for non-Latinx creators to make good TV and films about Latinxs. Even before Lee Unkrich (*Coco*, 2017) there were directors such as Karyn Kusama (*Girl Fight*, 2000) and Larry Clark (*Wassup Rockers*, 2005). For instance, in *Girl Fight* Kusama creates a film that delves into the complex life of a Latina whose life is straightjacketed by the restrictive gender roles enforced at home and within the community. We follow Diana (Michelle Rodriguez's breakout role) as she battles pressures to conform to old-school views on the place of Latinas (in the kitchen and at home taking care of the *familia*) and in the ring. And in Clark's *Wassup Rockers*, audiences learn that Latinxs are not just of Mexican, Cuban, Puerto Rican, or Dominican origin. Latinxs also include second-generation Central Americans (Guatemalan and Salvadoran). Moreover, he reminds audiences that Latinx teens today don't necessarily conform to a hip-hop and gang culture branding. His

Diana Guzman (played by Michelle Rodriguez) in *Girl Fight* (2000)

ragtag group of Latinxs wear skintight pants, listen to punk rock, play video games, and ride skateboards.

Building Puentes: Reel Latinx Niños

Latinx children as bridge makers between generations, linguistic communities, regional spaces, and more have seeped into the mainstream's reel imaginary in all sorts of ways. We saw this with California Milk Processor Board's commercial "La Llorona, Got Milk?"

The Latina is represented as a wispy woman ghost whose weeping stops momentarily when she opens a fridge and pulls out a carton of milk. She's had her *pan dulce* and is clearly in need of *leche* to wash it down. But the weeping starts again when she discovers that it's empty. Here the myth of La Llorona we heard as children weaves itself in and through the U.S. mediatized imagination: so that they wouldn't jump into the canals in and around their neighborhood in the northern California central valley, as children, Frederick and his friends were told the myth of the angry woman who hangs out by bodies of water and drowns children.

Many of the sitcoms we mentioned above rely on children and teens to be mainstream cultural interpreters for older-generation

California Milk Processor Board's commercial "La Llorona, Got Milk?" (2001)

Latinxs. This is such a characteristic feature of Latinx culture that we see this child-as-bridge function in all expressions of Latinx culture, including a majority of its literature. Piri Thomas's autobiography *Down These Mean Streets* (1967) is a powerful example of the way this can be an unbearable burden for kids. We see this in Latinx films, including the aforementioned runaway hit *Instructions Not Included* (*No se aceptan devoluciones*, 2013). That film builds much of its comedy around the translocated Mexican Valentín Bravo (Eugenio Derbez) and his cultural misunderstandings. He is saved by a new-generation Latinx, his daughter Maggie (Loreto Peralta), who *translates* Englishisms into Spanish and, as well, explains cultural differences. Indeed, reel and real Latinx kids tend to be placed as in-between figures, serving as bridges for older generations between their cultural and linguistic ties to their Latinx homelands on the one hand and to their new home in the United States on the other. These Latinx kids are a cultural, lingual, and epistemological bridge for others.

Niños and the Fantastical

Children's imagination is more abundant and fantastical than our adult variety. Magical realism has been a technique used in all variety of narrative formats—from literature to film to TV and more—as an envelope for articulating our culture, and often it's identified with the imagination of children.

Carlos "Carlitos" Reyes (played by Adrián Alonso) in *La misma luna* (2007)

In Patricia Riggan's *La misma luna* (2007), the child character, Carlitos (Adrián Alonso), manages to make his way across the dangerous U.S.-Mexico border and through the megalopolis of Los Angeles to find his mother (Rosario) on a street corner that he'd seen in his dreams.

Though Rosario and Carlitos miraculously find one another at this mystically foreseen L.A. street corner, given that the film unfolds largely from the point of view of a Latinx boy, perhaps we can be more forgiving.

Of course, not all magical realist reels are made alike. There's a long tradition of mainstream representations of Latinxs that situate us in some mysterious or otherworldly place, though it's important to note here that these otherworldly places are only rarely science fiction and fantasy modes of storytelling. Rather, Latinxs have been placed in stories of mystical, *curandismo*, shamanist, religious, or superstitious trappings on screen. A clear example of this is Mel Gibson's *Apocalypto*, which emphasizes ancient Mayan culture as bloodthirsty and violent. It ends with the arrival of European colonizers, a not-so-subtle signal that "civilization" and order had arrived to bring the indigenous peoples of America to heel as a means of saving them from themselves.

While many of us heard stories of La Llorona or even heard tell of the Incas, the Mayans, the Olmecs, the Aztecs—the ancestors of our forebears—the reel imaginary can and does *fix* us in some mystical past. In addition to Riggan's *La misma luna*, there's Alfonso Arau's film repertoire that includes *Como agua para chocolate* (1992) and *A Walk in the Clouds* (1995)—films that freeze us in distant, sepia-hued times and places.

On a side note, TV shows and film like to *naturalize* a sort of inherent link between Latinxs and superstition, or Latinxs and the mystical. While not a child, the twenty-something Ramone in HBO's *Here and Now* (2018) is a character somehow connected to visions; he's the one who exists as a kind of permeable barrier between the experiences of a Middle Eastern shrink. And in film we see this all the time. In fact, an example is director David Lynch's *Mullholland Drive*. At the gravitational center of the highbrow, auteur-driven pretzel narrative is Latina Rebecca del Rio, who performs as "la llorona de los angeles." She passes out, then dies on stage—for no reason. Latinidad is certainly not up front and center with Lynch, but it does provide him with a gossamer layer of mystery and mysticism.

Victoria Aragon (played by Aitana Sánchez-Gijón) and Paul Sutton (played by Keanu Reeves) in *A Walk in the Clouds* (1995)

Salsa is as ubiquitous in films and TV shows as ketchup these days. We've spiced up the average American's palette, but so has ketchup infiltrated the Latinx diet.

The plot of *Como agua para chocolate* (like the novel) unfolds as a series of recipes that lead to emotionally charged events. For instance, when protagonist Gertrudis, Tita's sister, eats a dish of quail in rose petal sauce, she rides off naked with a soldier on horseback into the sunset. The family ultimately disowns her.

Latinx food, in its quality or in cheapened, Taco Bell versions, has become such a part of the larger U.S. foodscape that it has almost taken on a life of its own. In film and TV, food culture has become an enormous signifier, almost a metonym, for Latinxs themselves. We believe that means that we will never go away. We see this in in Andy Tennant's *Fools Rush In* (1998) when the WASP character Alex Whitman (Mathew Perry) and love interest Isabel Fuentes (Salma Hayek) arrive at a family dinner. It's not only dinner that's being served, it's a full-blown fiesta. She tells him this is an average, normal dinner night with the *familia*. The house itself is chock full of Virgin Mary paintings, altars, and the usual Latinx bric-a-brac. Sometime after this meal with Isabel's *familia*, Whitman blurts out, "Somewhere between the tuna melts and your aunt's *tamales* I decided you're the one. I think we should get married right now." Once married, the film finds Isabel in the kitchen shaking her hips to Gloria Estefan while cooking for her white man.

For Jon Favreau, salvation and redemption come in the form of an authentic Cuban sandwich in his film *Chef* (2014). As Carl Casper, Favreau embodies the ennui of high-stakes food reviews, the pressure of attaining Michelin stars, and the unraveling personal life that often affect head chefs in the fine-dining industry.

Casper falls into disgrace, and his redemption can be attained only by returning to authentic, regional, cultural foods. His happiness, he realizes, comes in the form of a Cuban sandwich, the kind he remembers from growing up in Miami. As his personal relationships are healed, the film ends with Casper selling Cuban sandwiches from his food truck. Though the film is clearly a personal project for

Percy (played by Emjay Anthony) and Carl Casper (played by Jon Favreau) in *Chef* (2014)

Favreau (he wrote, produced, directed, and starred), the story would have made much more sense if Carl Casper were of Cuban ancestry. The film is basically about being jaded in a high-pressure career because one has forgotten one's roots. Favreau's character performs Latinidad, and Favreau as director does the same. The film is helped along with Latinx music, and Casper is aided by Latinx characters, played by John Leguizamo and Sofía Vergara. The only thing lacking is Casper's own apotheosis as a Cuban man, but the film remains a tale about how Latinx culture can be used to save a white man who experiences a nervous breakdown.

Anthony Lucero's (writer/director) *East Side Sushi* (HBO picked up and distributed it in 2015; now streamed on Amazon Prime) opens with the protagonist, Juana Martinez, waking up next to her *niña*, Lydia, early to prepare Lydia's breakfast and lunch. We quickly discover that she's a single *mamá* who is skilled at using leftovers from the fridge. Juana speaks English with her *niña*. But Juana's father, Apa, who lives at home, speaks only Spanish. Lucero cuts to a scene showing Juana and Apa cutting fruit, then putting it in containers they later sell at their street-corner fruit cart. Lucero's camera is careful to show details of the barrio. And those who know the streets and murals of

East Oakland, California, will recognize this as the story's location. As the narrative unfolds, we see how the preparation and eating of hybrid Asian and Mexican foods (e.g., sushi rolls with tortillas, chili, and shitake mushrooms) bring together otherwise segregated communities of color.

Associations with Latinxs and food occur in films such as *Como agua para chocolate* and *Fools Rush In*, but in less absurd and stereotypical ways in shows like *Cristela*, *Modern Family*, *Ugly Betty*, and María Ripoll's film, *Tortilla Soup*. In these and in Justin Lin's *Fast and Furious 6* (2013), we see the presence of food less as a reductive and essentialist move to represent our Latinoness. In these reconstructions, our tradition of food is revealed as a communal ritual and with *conversación de sobremesa* (when we discuss subjects in great detail and at great length after dinner). In *Cristela* human interaction doesn't so much take place around a sit-down meal as it does in a kitchen with characters grabbing food from the fridge, eating, then leaving. *Modern Family*'s creators appear to upend the stereotype of the Latina as somehow always affiliated with the domestic—Gloria doesn't cook—but it also might be reconstructing a current, more general trend in the United States that ritualized eating is no longer prevalent in the culture.

For instance, in *Ugly Betty*, the undocumented Latino father, Ignacio Suarez (Tony Plana), stays at home, cooks meals, and is primary caregiver to his two daughters. It is during dinners when the characters share their lives (including cousin Justin Suarez's coming out as gay) and the father shares his wisdom.

Tortilla Soup (2001) also features a Latinx papá (and widower) as the anchor in the home—and as the repository of cultural tradition generally. In this case Martin Naranjo (Héctor Elizondo) cooks elaborate Sunday meals for his three daughters, each struggling with life decisions (career and love life) that threaten to pull the family apart—and destroy their connection to their Latinx roots. While Ignacio Suarez is gentle and kind with his daughters, Martin is more of a macho, forbidding them to speak Spanglish at the table, for instance. Martin doesn't want them to speak Spanglish or to use both languages in the same sentence (code-shifting). As with *Ugly Betty*, all members of the Naranjo family are fluent in English and with mainstream culture.

However, there's a greater sense that the Naranjo daughters preserve more of the essential features of their Latinx culture, among them Mexican cuisine and the Spanish language.

Justin Lin ends *Fast and Furious 6* with the multicultural gang of speedsters sharing a meal at Dom Torreto's (Vin Diesel) house in East L.A. Six series into the franchise and Dom and his sister Mia's ethnicity are still not determined. However, that they sit around together as an ad hoc family becomes the marker of their Latinidad. This, and arguably the fact that Lin casts unmistakably Latina actresses such as Michelle Rodriguez and Brazilian soap star Jordana Brewster (also in Robert Rodriguez's *The Faculty* draped as Delilah Profitt), sends a message loud and clear: the Torretos aren't Italian American, they are Latinx.

The tradition of the Latinx *sobremesa*, that is, the time spent lingering and chatting after the meal, solidifies the Latinx family hierarchy: as head of the table, the individual adjudicates equitable food sharing and oversees the circulation of information, comments, and anecdotes. The figure presiding over the table can even regulate when and what is acceptable to speak about during eating time, what should be the right speed at which food is to be ingested, when and why one can be excused to leave the table, and so on. The *sobremesa* is a specific form of continuation of the family gathering within Latinx culture. Of course, this tradition is changing by the day. Statistical data show that families are no longer eating at the dinner table together on a regular basis. For economic reasons (many of us holding down multiple jobs to pay exorbitant mortgages or rents and with no fixed days for rest and long commutes) and as a result of other obligations, it's becoming increasingly impossible for families to meet every Sunday and share food, affection, and personal news together. It's becoming more and more difficult to enact this ritualized institution in Latinx culture (among others), where sharing food is confirmation of the family bond. Perhaps, then, Ripoll's making a point of showing us the *nopal* in the backyard of the Naranjo family home, which becomes a key ingredient in the father's dish in *Tortilla Soup*, functions more as a nostalgic move: a narrative gesture in tribute to the old days that we're losing as we move more and more into the quick, fast-food pace of contemporary life.

Getting food right in the reel reconstructions of Latinidad is important. One way or another, they structure family life in and around the preparing and eating of identifiably Latinx cuisine.

Latinx Representation Matters Wrap-Up

Forced passing and negation of one's Latinidad can and does have serious consequences. We see young Latinx children struggling with their own looks and identities as a result of the construction of a white imaginary. We see actors also struggling, and this from silver screen time immemorial. There's the case of Rita Hayworth (née Margarita Carmen Cansino) forced to pluck eyebrows and be a more consumable silver-screen Latina, who eventually turned to drink. Similarly, *made-over* early silver-screen star Lupe Vélez committed suicide by overdosing and jamming her head down a toilet. Most recently, Demi Lovato had to check into a rehab clinic for depression, cutting, eating disorders, and drugs after nearly overdosing.

LET'S TALK GENDER AND SEXUALITY

Polarized Reconstructions of Latinas

We're certainly living in a different televisual, silver-screen epoch than in the days of Rita Hayworth and Lupe Vélez, but when we look at the writing and casting of Latinas today, not a lot seems to have changed. Vélez, Hayworth, Carmen Miranda, and other early Latina stars were relegated to playing very limited roles that emphasized their sexuality above nearly everything else. Lupe Vélez was known as the Mexican Spitfire, a moniker mainstream TV and film seem to hang around the necks of Sofía Vergara, Jennifer Lopez, Eva Mendes, Eva Longoria, Salma Hayek, and others. A quick case in point: in *Chicago Hope* (1996) Jennifer Lopez cameoed as a teenager with gonorrhea of the throat; we already discussed earlier in this book her hypersexed music videos. We think, too, of the roles Eva Mendes plays, including Roxanne "Roxy" Simpson in *Ghost Rider* (2007).

She's never shown *without* low-cut tops and full cleavage, usually draped all over Nicholas Cage. And when Latinas are simply strong-of-mind characters, they often also slip into the whore side of the virgin-whore binary. In *The Women* Mendes is so sexually out of control that she can't stop herself from sleeping with a married man—even after the man and his wife ask her to stop. While Carmen Miranda and Lupe Vélez *were* the only Latina representations on the silver screen in their time and

Roxanne "Roxy" Simpson (played by Eva Mendes) in *Ghost Rider* (2007)

today we have dozens more on our screens, when it comes to the reel reconstruction of Latinas, the twenty-first century seems to mirror hypersexualized reconstructions of the silent and Technicolor eras.

Set against this long history of reconstructing Latinas as spitfires, there was the equally strong impulse to write and cast Latinas as docile and asexual or virginal. We already mentioned earlier in the book how Paz Vega was cast as the passive, naïve, virginal Mexican émigré maid Flor Moreno in *Spanglish* (2004). There's also, of course, *Ugly Betty*, which portrays the Latina virgin straight and in formulaic ways.

The mainstream isn't solely to blame here. Latinx culture has a long, deep history of setting up this division between the virgin and the whore. It's the basis of myths and childhood stories such as La Llorona—a proverbial whore who not only betrays her man for another man but drowns her children in order to get the other man; it's the reason that history books in Mexico and beyond have identified the super smart Nahua woman Malintzin (or Doña Marína), who was enslaved and then served as translator and lover to Hernán Cortés as La Malinche. To this day, *malinchesta* pejoratively identifies a disloyal woman. This is why we see this virgin-saint versus whore-malinche paradigm so deeply embedded in Latinx culture across the Americas. The sexualization of Latinas in telenovelas is a case in point.

We see this especially pronounced in the *narconovelas*. For instance, in Colombia there are the *narconovelas*, of which *El cártel*, *El capo* (The boss), and *Sin tetas no hay paraíso* (Without tits there is no paradise) are salient examples. *Sin tetas no hay paraíso* went through two different versions in Colombia, where it became the most watched soap opera and was to be adapted for NBC in the United States, a project soon abandoned. In Spain, Telecinco bought the story line from Caracol Televisión and adapted it to local conditions. All versions follow essentially the same story of a young girl who becomes a prostitute after joining a gang of drug traffickers. In all these instances, we see how the stories rely on the amalgam of the virgin-whore figure within the context of narco narratives. In the Latin American context, these kinds of shows compete with many different televisual narratives that have Latin Americans in a host of roles. But pluck out the narco- and human-trafficking story and drop it into a TV landscape, where there are not as many stories with Latinxs in them, and we have an instant stereotype.

Stepping back to the U.S. context, we do have film and TV narratives that foreground this polarization of Latinas as virgins or whores. We think again of María Ripoll's film *Tortilla Soup*, discussed in the last chapter. The film makes clear how the virgin-whore dichotomy operates in our families. The older sister Leticia (Elizabeth Peña) appears in white clothes, prays as a devout Catholic, saves herself for marriage, and reminds the others of cultural traditions. The middle sister, Carmen (Jacqueline Obradors), wears dark clothes, seems distant from her cultural roots, and has sex for the sake of having sex. And the creators of *Jane the Virgin* are smart about this amalgam stereotype, creating a show about Latinas that's entirely emplotted by the virgin-whore dichotomy.

Of course, this is not unique to Latinx culture. We see this same polarization of women in European patriarchal societies generally. Think Salem Witch Trials in the United States. Think J. R. R. Tolkien, *The Lord of the Rings*, with its untouchable goddesses and fearful women. Galadriel sometimes is perceived as both. With some exceptions (as we mentioned with *Jane the Virgin*, which seems wholly aware of this disquieting tradition), Hollywood and prime-time TV play an outsized role in making this virgin-whore polarity indelible and lasting.

This formula is a lazy version of reel re-creations of Latinas and women generally, and it persists. We can do more than speculate here. With the #MeToo movement and women's struggles generally behind and in front of cameras, there's inequality on all levels. There still persists a largely patriarchal structure that determines roles and who plays them. More pointedly, it's straight, white guys who occupy the seats—pitching, writing, directing, awarding. And these straight, white guys are comforted and reassured when they see these exaggerations of women. When they think of their mothers, sisters, daughters, they imagine them only as saints and virgins; when they think of women they desire, they think only spitfire, whore. Combine that with the history of the Latina spitfire or bombshell and, as their track record proves, these straight, white guys can't seem to think outside these simplistic representations of women that reduce them to either passive virgin or out-of-control sexpot.

The virgin-whore dichotomy that pervades reel reconstructions of Latinas is not only offensive and shameful, it is dangerous. One way or another, it etches deeper and deeper the idea (belief, myth) that women are responsible for the sexual advances they receive. It is the way a woman behaves, her figure, the way she dresses, the eye contact she makes that are responsible for how men behave—*not how successful men are at keeping their hands to themselves!* We know men are the ones who should be taught, as young boys, how to respect women and control themselves. But our society has historically put the blame on women, and the virgin-whore reel reconstructions further deepen this belief.

Perhaps we would guess that Latinxs like Vergara, Hayek, Mendes, Longoria, and others are so successful that they surely have more control over the roles they choose and how they inhabit them. We would presume that since Longoria and Vergara are some of the highest-paid actors on TV, they should be able to pick and choose. Eva Longoria created *Devious Maids*, recreated for U.S. audiences from the Mexican soap opera *Ellas son la alegría del hogar* (They are the joy of the home). All the Latinas in *Devious Maids* speak heavily Spanish-accented English, wear low-cut tops, and relish their bodies and their sexuality. It's even more over the top than Gloria in *Modern Family.*

There's a scene when Zoila Diaz (Judy Reyes from *Scrubs*) is about to begin an affair with her boss, daytime soap star Spence Westmore. She's a maid, but one who's dressed more for a nightclub than cleaning floors. And when he makes advances on her in front of his baby, Zoila hits him over the head with a pan. *Devious Maids* is filled with clichés. Critics like us might try to rescue the show, arguing that it's cliché ridden for a purpose—precisely to push into the foreground the kind of representations of Latinas that have existed and that continue to do so. After all, could its producer, Eva Longoria, who received a degree in Chicano/a Studies from Cal State Northridge, back a TV show that uncritically reproduces stereotypes of Latinas? But we are reminded that the clichés in *Devious Maids* aren't signposted, so we know they are gross stereotypes. And the show does nothing to undo or satirize them. The target audience doesn't appear to be asked to regard these stereotypes with contempt. Rather, the audience is asked to revel in these stereotypes and not in a very interesting way. The show does nothing to dispel the virgin-whore stereotype; actually, it drives it deeper into the U.S. audience psyche. The same applies to Jennifer Lopez, of course. Yet, and we mentioned this in passing already, Jennifer Lopez's song and video "Booty" and "I luh ya papi" are straight-male-gaze pornographic.

Within the mainstream trend to hypersexualize Latinas, there's a simultaneous desire *and* fear of Latinas; that somehow the Latina (a kind of *vagina dentate*) will chew up and spit out the straight, white guy audience (execs, creators, and men in the seats). It participates in the Latinx threat narrative: *swarms* of Latinxs taking jobs, using resources, soiling white America with incivilities. It's the bedrock of ideologies that backed slavery and later Jim Crow and that still operate today to give Anglos the opportunity to imagine the bodies of women of color as at once desirous and forbidden as ordained by God, same God who seemed to tell whites that it was okay to commit acts of genocide in the slave trade triangle and in the manifest destiny to expand westward. This racist ideology supported not only righteous justifications for genocide but also the sexualization, possession, and rape of the bodies of women of color. Conversely, white women were coded as virginal, and their pure bodies had to be protected at all costs. A central scaffold to the erecting of this racist ideology was the coding of black and brown men of this country as lechers and rapists, sexual monsters who had to be kept at bay or even destroyed just as one would a wild animal.

This continues to permeate our cinematic and televisual imaginary in the United States. Onscreen, as we've been discussing, the early history was to cast Latinas as sex crazed, almost primal creatures who were ruled (and thus could be tamed) by their sexual urges. Latinas, then, were out-of-control sexual creatures unless that one man, a white man, of course, could subdue them. It's a racist, sexist ideology that feeds into the she-was-asking-for-it rationale used in defense of sexual assault and rape. It's the simultaneous desire *and* fear of Latinas that undergirds

Christopher Marshall (played by Ralph Fiennes) and Marisa Ventura (played by Jennifer Lopez) in *Maid in Manhattan* (2002)

much of film and TV representations of empowered Latinas as somehow aggressive sexual creatures. It's why we have so many versions
of that *Maid in Manhattan* narrative we discuss earlier in the book,
where it's the *civilized* white guy (*British* Ralph Fiennes) who *tames*
the Latina (U.S. Latinx Jennifer Lopez).

This happens, seemingly, even in other planetary systems. James
Cameron introduced innovations into the film-viewing experience
with the awe-inspiring 3D of *Avatar* (2009) but slipped right back
into this desire/fear mode of reconstructing Latinas by creating Trudy
Chacon (Michelle Rodriguez), geared up in her military fatigues with
just enough cleavage and piloting heavily weaponized planes in contrast with the lithe and naked (blue-painted) Zoe Saldana as Neeytiri.
Here again the white guy (Sam Worthington as Jake Sully) saves the
indigenous peoples and gets his Pocahontas-like trophy for his efforts.

Indeed, Zoe Saldana's casting history has been one that pivots
between the proverbial virgin and whore stereotypes. Saldana made
her cinematic debut as Latinx Eva Rodriguez in *Center Stage* (2000).
She's street, sassy, and all body—she's a dancer.

By the time we see her in Olivier Megaton's *Colombiana* (2011),
she's all body, but now a scantily clad skilled assassin hell bent on
avenging the murder of her parents. As self-realized, Batman-like superhero (her origin story includes shots of her training to become a
badass), her skills at pummeling the bad guys measure up with the

Cataleya Restrepo (played by Zoe Saldana) in *Colombiana* (2011)

best of them, but there are one too many scenes where the camera forgets she even has a face.

It's mostly interested in showing her wet (sweaty) brown body in tank tops and underwear—even her sucking on lollipops. Laura Mulvey called this the "male gaze," the persistence of the camera eye to fixate and linger on sexualized aspects of the woman's body on screen. To be an action hero, Cataleya has to be skimpily clad.

While we will be discussing sci-fi in the next chapter, we'd like to mention Zoe Saldana's roles in the *Guardians of the Galaxy* and *Star Trek* films here. As both Gamora and Uhura, Saldana brings power and self-assuredness to the roles. Gamora is the adopted (and favored) daughter of the Mad Titan, Thanos, in the Marvel Universe. As a vital character in the Marvel Cinematic Universe, Gamora is a compelling character for both her complexity and feminist sensibilities. She is self-sufficient and smart and can be read as instrumental in the effort to disrupt the patriarchal rule of Thanos, who literally killed half of Gamora's civilization and "adopted" her. The drawback to Gamora and Saldana's portrayal of her is that Gamora is green skinned, which means that Saldana, as she was in *Avatar*, is masked by paint. Her naturally brown pigmented skin is obscured, and at least one of her signifiers—perhaps the most prominent in the visually dominant medium of film—is erased.

On the other hand, as Uhura, the character famously originated by Nichelle Nichols in the original *Star Trek* TV series, she is not painted over. However, because Nichols is African American, it is generally understood that Uhura is of African heritage. This fact results in a problematic rendering of Uhura as played by Saldana.

Because Saldana has an Afro-Latina phenotype, she is able to pass as African American in many of the roles she plays. Here, just as a light-skinned Latina can erase her Latinidad in a role that is coded as white, Afro-Latinx actors make the same thing happen when they can pass as black.

Nyota Uhura (played by Zoe Saldana) in *Star Trek Beyond* (2016)

Saldana is yet another example of the fluidity of the Latinx phenotype that has grand consequences when it comes to the issue of cultural and racial representation on screen.

Brown *Mamás*

In *Maid in Manhattan* Jennifer Lopez's a single *mamá*. In Alan Poul's *The Back-up Plan* (2010) she plays Zoe, whose drive to become a *mamá* is so deep that she does away with men altogether, at least initially. She undergoes artificial insemination. Her brown *mamá* autonomy, however, is thrown out the back door as her life becomes more and more entangled with the Anglo character, Stan (Alex O'Loughlin). The film ends with them coupled and, after a shot of her pushing their twins in a perambulator along with their paraplegic dog, Nuts, there's a shot of her suddenly overcome with morning sickness, the promise of another baby on the way. In another of her über*mamá* roles in the film *Enough* (2002), she portrays the character Slim, who is hell bent on protecting herself and her daughter from her husband's physical abuse. She becomes über*mamá* when she learns self-defense methods, transforming her from prey to predator. Lopez takes matters into her own hands in a more direct, physically demanding way. The creators do well to imagine her not just as an emotionally and psychologically strong woman but a *physically* strong woman. And in TV shows we see the same. For instance, in *Jane the Virgin*, Jane's *mamá* is single and struggling.

In the 2016 TV series *Shades of Blue* (2016–2017), Jennifer Lopez plays the role of Harlee Santos, a corrupted cop and single *mamá*. The creators of the show depict her as duplicitous, a traitor, and a murderer.

It's not that our communities don't have single Latinx *mamás*. Of course we do. However, we ask what kind of ideal audience these creators have in mind when

Harlee Santos (played by Jennifer Lopez) in *Shades of Blue* (season 2, episode 2, 2017)

reconstructing the Latinx *mamá*? Some of these films are romantic comedies and thrillers, so we should expect less of the male-gazing camera lens. Jennifer Lopez's certainly not geared up as if she's in a wet–T-shirt contest or shot seductively sucking a lollipop. Yet when we strip it all down, whether we talk gritty cop show or rom-com, the Latina-as-*mamá* stereotype just keeps piling up.

There are a few films that seem to get it more right concerning the reconstruction of Latina *mamá*s. For instance, in Gregory Nava's *Bordertown* (2006), Jennifer Lopez transforms from a stylish *güera* journalist investigating the rapes and murders (*femicides*) on the Mexican side of the U.S.-Mexico border into a boots-on-the-street super-*mamá* who cares for all the girls, including especially an escapee, Eva (Maya Zapata). She defies a patriarchal system of cops and even fellow journalists (Martin Sheen as her boss, George Morgan, and Antonio Banderas as Mexican journalist Dias) that are in one way or another complicit in the murder and rape of these women. She puts herself in danger (the case is about the murders of Latinx women), and she soon realizes that the problem, and consequently the threat, is systemic. The film makes visible the patriarchal structures that help motivate violence against women, and Lopez does a good job in selling the role without becoming the mother figure, which is what a patriarchal system would lead her toward.

Brown Mammies

Latinas have been featured as the brown nanny, and not just by non-Latinxs. We mentioned in the last chapter how Alejandro González Iñárritu had Adriana Barraza gain thirty-five pounds for her role as the nanny, Amelia, to the blond children of Mr. and Mrs. Jones (Brad Pitt and Cate Blanchett). We also mentioned how mainstream reconstructions often depict Latinxs as Other, doing all the work, such as raising children, cleaning, and so forth, and then the Anglos taking all the credit. The United States has gotten too comfortable seeing Latinas as nannies and surrogate parents or as maids and cleanup crews. We need our Latinx version of the iconic scene in *Forrest Gump* where whites are serving Bubba's mother after the scene with Bubba's mother serving a white family. These types of role reversals help to undo entrenched stereotypes of Latinxs as workers and servants.

Let's not forget the reel instances when Latinas take control of the way the media has depicted them as *mamás* or otherwise. For instance, there's Kat Von D, whose tattoos of different Latina figures all over her body—from her mother to Lupe Vélez, among others—can be seen as a reclamation and affirmation of her Latinidad. Her tattooed body can also be read as Kat Von D's way to challenge the "aesthetics of the exoticized Latina body," as scholar Theresa Rojas puts it.

We recognize that in the case of Kat Von D, who is light skinned and ambiguously Latina, the danger of marking her body might not be as great as if she were dark and mestizo. She plays herself on her reality shows, or at least a persona of herself. Until she announces her Latinidad through her body art or appears in magazines where she discusses her heritage, she can easily pass as white.

Status and money also figure strongly in protecting Latinas. Jennifer Lopez's socioeconomic position in the 1 percent makes her able to take risks. Thus, in her music video "I luh ya papi" she can be the one to control the camera gaze. The video opens with an Anglo music video producer suggesting that it be made in a zoo, a carnival, or a water park. Then, after she pokes fun at all this with her backup dancers—"Why do the men always objectify the women?"—Lopez shifts to a fantasy where the dangers are themselves agents of the gaze. She can pair up with Iggy's derriere and make a music video like "Booty," which, in its hyperbolic gazing of their derrieres, arguably inverts the male gaze. And yet we also know that these music video narratives are playing it safe. They don't *really* undo patriarchy and the predominance of the male gaze. We hold up Beyoncé's *Lemonade*, which does manage to offer a sustained effort to speak to issues of masculinity and what it means to strive toward a feminist ideal.

Jennifer Lopez does have her Beyoncé moment, however. In Gregory Nava's *Selena* (1997), Jennifer Lopez's morphology matches pretty well that of the singer she portrays, Selena Quintanilla. More importantly, it isn't the dramatic realization of Jennifer Lopez's butt that the camera is interested in. It is in the telling of the story of this important Latina crossover artist (both into Mexico and into the United States). Jennifer Lopez as Selena and the telling of Selena's story posthumously put Selena on the radar of the U.S. mainstream since many outside of the Spanish-speaking Latinx community were unfamiliar with her. Moreover, this role helped make Jennifer Lopez better known as an actor; it was her true breakout moment in film and the first film in which she received top billing.

In addition to Jennifer Lopez, we think of Salma Hayek in the 2002 biopic *Frida* as something of a resistant role. Here the stereotypical reel Latina body (Hayek) is portrayed as a pained, disabled body. This, too, was a turning point for Hayek's career,

Selena (played by Jennifer Lopez) in *Selena* (1997)

not only because it was a dramatic role but also because Kahlo's body itself was a liability. For an actress so well known for her physical attributes, this lack of bodily agency imbues her performance of Frida Kahlo with extraordinary power. The role earned Hayek a Best Actress Oscar nomination in 2003 (she lost to Nicole Kidman for *The Hours*).

Frida Kahlo (played by Salma Hayek) in *Frida* (2002)

Karyn Kusama's *Girlfight* (2000) features Michelle Rodriguez as the stubborn Latina teen Diana Guzmán, who chooses amateur boxing rather than a domesticated Latina gender role. She's treated as a kind of traitor to her family—her father, Sandro (Paul Calderón), and others in her Brooklyn tenement. Rodriguez/Guzman goes against Latinx *machista* familial norms and is labeled a malinche figure. Aware of this, the film in its writing and camera treatments empower her decisions to break the mold, to make her more than just a Latina with a body but a Latina with a mind of her own.

Michelle Rodriguez's acting itself resists being simple-mindedly sexualized. Justin Lin's camera tries to hypersexualize her in the *Fast and Furious* franchise. But when she's seen draped over Dom, or when he helps her find her memories of their romance and then touching the scars on her body, she resists these eroticizing moments through her facial expression and her body language. She exists outside of these easily categorized types in which Latinas tend to appear. She's sexualized, but she also exudes a kind of defiant femininity. She's independent, spirited, willing to grimace or cast a dismissive glance and body posture. She resists the will of the camera's eye and the director to eroticize and sexualize her.

Robert Rodriguez exploits this aspect of Michelle Rodriguez in his casting of her as Shé in *Machete* (2010). She wears a sports-bra top and a machine gun, an eye patch and a grimace, all while complicating the eroticized gaze. Michelle Rodriguez is an attractive woman with beautiful features and an athletic figure. Yet she retains that element of control over her sexuality even when she's in a sports top. She may be unique in this. We can't think of another Latina who can accomplish the same thing. Put Jennifer Lopez in a sports bra while wearing an eye patch and holding a machine gun, and that's truly ridiculous. On the other hand, place Michelle Rodriguez in a video like "Booty," and it doesn't work.

Shé (played by Michelle Rodriguez) in *Machete* (2010)

Casting against Typification

Robert Rodriguez built a film career by casting Latinas who resist typification. We think readily of Salma Hayek's transformation from Latina seductress to the monstrous queen vampire Satánico Pandemónium in *From Dusk till Dawn* (1996).

She becomes exactly the seductress/witch type with which women, and especially Latinas, are associated. Rodriguez presents the male-gazing camera eye by introducing her dancing and the men in the bar ogling her, then flips this on its head when she morphs into a snake-like human-hybrid vampire. It's Rodriguez's Latina biting back. He does something similar with Jessica Alba's role of Sartana in *Machete*. She undergoes a transformation from *pocha* (sellout) *migra* field agent to self-acting, autonomous Latina.

Satánico Pandemónium (played by Salma Hayek) in *From Dusk till Dawn* (1996)

Latinas in Complex Technicolor Color

In *Latinas and Latinos on TV*, Isabel Molina-Guzmán uses the concept of color-conscious writing to identify shows such as *Scrubs* (2001–2010). Here, the creators write the Latina character Carla Espinosa (Judy Reyes) as more than just hot tempered and sassy. She's smart, strong willed, and disruptive of misinformed narratives about Latinidad. While characters try to make her the butt of ethnic or gendered jokes, she turns these attempts inside out. In a scene where her husband, the African American character Christopher Turk (Donald Faison), can't recall her heritage, we see her take hold of racial and ethnic identity markers in ways that actively disrupt the simplifying and fixing of Latina identity. Television viewers know (over the eight seasons) that she's of Dominican origin and migrated and grew up in Chicago because she constantly makes her fellow workers aware of this. Turk's and others' attempts to pigeonhole her as something else (Mexican or Puerto Rican) and not Dominican blatina call into question the mainstream's oversimplification of Latinoness generally. She constantly disrupts mainstream, non-Latinx audiences' idea that all Latinxs who appear on screen are of Mexican descent largely because the media has historically lumped us all together and because nearly three-quarters of all Latinxs in the United States are of Mexican ancestry. Having Carla Espinosa take the moment to educate Turk as the stand-in for a non-Latinx majority audience about the fact that not all Latinxs are from the same area underscores the need to undo reel histories that homogenized Latinx culture.

Latina Redemption Narratives

In many reconstructions of Latinas coded as bad, disloyal, or "loose," there's also present a path to redemption—and this usually through marriage. Returning to our earlier discussion of *Fools Rush In*, we see how the creators at first code the Latina Isabel Fuentes as temptress: she wears the bad-girl black leather jacket and is the one responsible for the one-night stand that leads to her pregnancy. When she tells her family, they aren't surprised that she got knocked up out of wedlock. However, setting herself on a path that ultimately leads to her marrying the white protagonist, Alex Whitman, offers this possibility of redemption—to her family and to moviegoing audiences. The film offers the possibility of salvation for the *puta* figure if she's willing to commit the rest of her life to monogamous devotion and submission to the patriarchal institution of marriage and family making. She's transformed from bad to good as a married Latina *mamá*. We see this redemption narrative with much of the writing of roles for Latinas that fill prime-time TV screens. While *Jane the Virgin* breaks new ground in terms of its nearly entire Latinx cast and writers, and it innovates in the way that Jane is the agent of the story itself in a metafictional way, in the end it's also this redemption narrative. She's knocked up (artificially and by accident) and unmarried. However, Jane's honesty, holding out for marriage before sex, her hard work as hotel maid and part-time Catholic school teacher, and her studying to finish her degree ultimately promise redemption.

Latinas Working the Industry

It's a fact that the TV industry is making money off of Latinas. It's also a fact that some of these Latinas are themselves making money—and lots of it. Already in 2012, Sofía Vergara was the highest-paid actress on TV, raking in approximately $19 million a year; she's kept the top spot as the highest-paid (and wealthiest) Latina actor ever since. Eva Longoria was ranked third. In 2017, Jennifer Lopez's net worth was in the $360 million range. They might be uncritically reproducing stereotypes, but they certainly have become wealthy doing so.

Not all Latinas are Sofía Vergara, Eva Longoria, or Jennifer Lopez, however. Jennifer Lopez built a career that goes beyond her dancing (she began as a dancer on the comedy sketch show *In Living Color*) into the areas of music, videos, films, TV, and even professional sports (there was a time when she and ex-husband, singer and actor Marc Anthony, were part owners of the Miami Dolphins). In the end, she and other Latinxs have the right and privilege to play against or into stereotypes. But by the same token, critics of culture and all things Latinx, like the authors of this book, have a duty and an obligation to examine and analyze the implications of the choices these Latinas make in the form of the roles they portray on screen.

We're against censoring. We are also against silence on the subject of these stereotypes and impactful representations on the screen.

Latina™

Vergara has underwear and makeup lines; Longoria's a producer of TV shows like *Devious Maids*, *Telenovela*, and *Crowded*. Jennifer Lopez no longer has to be identified by her full name. We know her simply by the trademark J.Lo. In each case, these Latina actors have become consumable commodities for others to try on, buy, and wear. They have turned parts of themselves into reified objects. They are turning huge profits on their representations as virgins, whores, malinches, and everything in between. But these are but a few Latinas who are doing so. Most Latinas are just regular everyday folks but who have to suffer the consequences of the circulation of these images. As we've been discussing throughout this book, Latinx stereotypes and their commodified circulation have deleterious effects on society when there is little else to counter them. We would be less apprehensive about these Latina stereotypes if we had a greater abundance of fuller, more complex representations as well.

Wrapping Up with Latinx-Queer Resistance

Yesteryear's prime-time LGBTQ Latinx characters were largely unseen, functioned as comic relief, or simply existed as hyperexaggerated stereotypes. In the much-lauded *Will and Grace* (1998–2006), Will's partner, Vince D'Angelo, could have been written as a Latinx

character; he's played by Italian Cuban actor Bobby Cannavale.

Creators of the all-lesbian show *The L Word* (2004–2009) cast Indian Dutch American Janina Zione Gavanker as the Latina woman-whore Eva "Papi" Torres and Iranian American Sarah Shahi as the Latina Carmen de la Pica Morales, ditched at the alter by Shane. We already discussed how Óscar Martínez on NBC's *The Office* (2005–2012) was depicted as the office punching bag, both as Latinx and as gay.

Vince D'Angelo (played by Bobby Cannavale) kissing Will Truman (played by Eric McCormack) in *Will and Grace* (season 7, episode 5, 2004)

What we've seen in reel narratives is a history of double and triple marginalization when it comes to LGBTQ characters. They are marginalized for their sexuality, often becoming the punching bag or punch-line figure. And as Latinx characters they are straightjacketed by ethnoracial and cultural stereotypes.

This said, there are some interesting new TV shows that complicate this reel landscape. The creators of *True Blood* have a gay Latinx brujo (witch) character Jesus Velasquez (Kevin Alejandro) who is in a relationship with gay African American psychic (medium who can contact ghosts) Lafayette Reynolds (Nelsan Ellis). Jesus is killed off, however, in the season 4 finale. The creators also have another Latinx character, skinwalker Luna Garza (Janina Gavankar), who can take the shape of (pass as) other humans. The show kills off both characters, but their appearance told TV viewers that Latinxs can be queer and fantastically other, just like white characters.

In the Netflix series *Orange Is the New Black* (2013–) we encounter many different LGBTQ Latina characters. As season 7 unfolds, the narrative moves the voice and agency from the Anglo, Piper Chapman (Taylor Schilling), to the Latinas. We're thinking of Dayanara "Daya" Diaz (Dascha Polanco), who starts a relationship with the androgynous drug dealer Daddy in season 6.

We are also thinking of the bilingual, hyperliterate, witty best friends Maritza Ramos (played by Diane Guerrero) and Marisol "Flaca" Gonzales (played by Jackie Cruz). This diversity occurs within a prison narrative—a carceral space that's supposed to rehabilitate inmates but doesn't. While we might ask whether this is the only space in which TV can imagine a great variety of Latina subjects, we also see how the show writes these Latinas as modern-day tricksters who operate just askew of the center to reveal deep truths about the sociopolitical underbelly of the prison system and global capitalism generally.

Daya Diaz (played by Dascha Polanco) in *Orange is the New Black* (season 5, episode 1, 2017)

Fantasy and prison story worlds are not the only reel story-world spaces that are at once permissible mainstream spaces for LGBTQ Latinx subjects and places of resistance. There's also sci-fi.

For instance, in CBS's *Star Trek: Discovery* (2017–), Bryan Fuller (of *American Gods*) and Alex Kurtzman cast gay blatinx actor Wilson Cruz (he played Latinx-queer *avant la lettre* Enrique "Rickie" Vasquez in ABC's mid-1990s *My So-Called Life*) as gay Dr. Hugh Culber. Here, again, we see how the mainstream makes *permissible* the queer Latinx subject by giving Wilson Cruz's character a French-sounding last name, erasing any Latinx that might have informed his role. Yet there's an element of resistance if we consider that the show has Cruz as Culber appear *out* with his partner, astronomycologist Paul Stamets (Anthony Rapp). Episode 5 (53 minutes into the show) ends with the two of them brushing their teeth, talking, and gently touching one another as they ready for bed. And in episode 9 Stamets tells Culber, "I love you." Culber reciprocates with the same. They kiss—and in medium close-up.

Chapter 6

LATINXS IN REEL SPECULATIVE SPACES

Lay of the Extraterrestrial Land

We both love our sci-fi—and especially these days when Latinxs are making a few (albeit brief) appearances in the built other worlds of *Star Wars*. In *Rogue One* Jimmy Smits, as Senator Bail Organa of Alderaan (who appears in *The Phantom Menace, Attack of the Clones, Revenge of the Sith*), makes a few momentary appearances along with Diego Luna as the smart, fierce Cassian Andor. And with Guatemalan Latinx actor Oscar Isaac as Poe Dameron, we even had a continuity of character over two installments: *The Force Awakens* (2015) and *The Last Jedi* (2017). And let's not forget the casting of Benicio del Toro as the duplicitous DJ in *The Last Jedi*.

Speculative genres potentially allow for a more capacious and imaginative re-creation of the building blocks of reality. They offer the possibility for creators to think of ways that Latinxs, for instance, can be reimagined in a future or fantasy world that may or may not have to do with our present condition.

However, speculative reel narratives have a long history of *absenting* Latinxs. It's as if the creators (mostly white) simply don't see us in the present quotidian world. That is, creators working in the speculative genres exercise their *counterfactual* processes to distill from our present day and then imagine and recreate elaborate story worlds that consider the various consequences (plot) of different thought experiments to transport audiences into these hypothetical projections toward the futurescapes. However, as the distillation and reconstruction processes from the building blocks of reality take place, Latinxs (in spite of our rapidly increasing demographic numbers) are absented.

Stanley Kubrick's *2001: A Space Odyssey* (1968) is another case in point. There is no reason why Dave Bowman (the human astronaut who must tangle with the supercomputer HAL 9000 and ultimately achieve an interstellar rebirth as the Star Child) could not have been a Latinx character played by a Latinx actor. Yet Kubrick (along with author Arthur C. Clarke) cast an Anglo actor, Keir Dullea. We see the same thing decades later with the time-space sci-fi *Interstellar* (2014), where director Christopher Nolan and his creative team assembled a nearly all white cast—and this in a twenty-first-century production. One could argue that their distillation and reconstruction of the building blocks of reality mirror one that doesn't often include Latinxs in national space and astronaut programs. Yet we can and do still hold them accountable for failing to use their counterfactual capacity to imagine anything but Anglo characters in space. As with James Cameron, these titans of imagination and creative exploration didn't use their counterfactual mechanisms to think *outside the box*. We can ask George Lucas, Why was Luke Skywalker not Latinx? There is nothing about the character that says he must be played by a white actor. When creators do see and then distill Latinxs to imagine us in distant times and places, as we already mentioned of James Cameron's slipping into the tired Pocahontas formula with *Avatar*, it's simplistic at best.

In *Elysium* (2013) Neill Blomkamp chooses to depict Earth as a massive shanty/favela filled with brown people. The film's earthbound scenes were shot in a dump in the poor Iztapalapa district on the outskirts of Mexico City, while the scenes for Elysium were shot in Vancouver and the wealthy Huixquilucan-Interlomas suburbs of Mexico City.

Latinxs are present, but in ways in which the film narrative locates issues of overpopulation and pollution in the brown subject.

Julio (played by Diego Luna), Max Da Cost (played by Matt Damon), and Spider (played by Wagner Moura) in *Elysium* (2013)

And Blomkamp reverts to the white-savior (Matt Damon) protagonist formula. It is a dystopian view of the future in which Latinxs are left behind and the wealthy have all the benefits their wealth can buy. We acknowledge that, but the rest of the film engages with Latinxs as an important and valuable part of our society. Latinxs are present and, moreover, we are worth saving. In contrast to our invisibility in so many other speculative spaces of the future, we rather appreciate what Blomkamp does here. Our presence, even if depicted as wretched but in progress, is necessary. We should always applaud that.

Notably, too, this speculative straightjacketing of Latinxs isn't just in story worlds that reach forward in time; we see this same stereotyping when it reaches back in time. A case in point would be Don Chaffey's *One Million Years B.C.* (1966), which features Raquel Welch (née Jo Raquel Tejada) as deer-skinned, bikini-clad Loana the Fair One as the überprogenitrix of *Homo sapiens sapiens*.

Theorist Frederic Jameson talks about the failure of the imagination with sci-fi as evidence that creators lack the capacity to imagine the future as anything but an extrapolation of the most barbaric forms of capitalism and as evidence of systemic cultural-ideological closure. This is a multilayered failure

Loana the Fair One (played by Raquel Welch) in *One Million Years B.C.* (1966)

if we add into the mix the long trend of non-Latinx creators making racially monochromatic futurescapes that erase and/or alienate the significant presence of Latinxs.

To state this otherwise, it is easy to get swept up in an engaging narrative about a future or alternate world or about voyaging across the vastness of interstellar space or any of the other imagined, fantastical worlds and focus only on how distinct the world is from our own. Yet it is actually the reverse. These fantastical worlds are rooted in our present-day reality; that is why they remain recognizable to audiences. Reel speculative story worlds can go only so far away from our own human experiences before they suddenly make no sense to us. We would no longer recognize ourselves within such a fictive setting. As it pertains to Latinxs in the United States, if we continue to see a surging Latinx demographic, it should make sense that Latinxs begin to appear more regularly in speculative films and TV shows. Our reality affects the imagined stories we tell. It cannot be otherwise.

Extrapolation or Appropriation?

It appears that it's easier for Anglo directors to build speculative possible worlds by appropriating aspects of another culture and "reimagining" them in a speculative context. Lucas had a habit of doing this in recasting cultural totems of Mexican and Japanese culture. Lucas fed his imagination by dipping into and appropriating iconic images from hemispheric Latinx and other national cultures. It's no secret that the Jedi are based on the *jidaigeki*, which are dramas about samurai. Chewbacca, whose nickname, spelled Chewie, sounds exactly like the diminutive for Jesús (Chuy). As a pistolero he wears what looks exactly like a Mexican bandolier worn by Mexican revolutionaries. However, as we've mentioned earlier in this book, Latinx audiences aren't passive sponges of reel reconstructions of Latinxs. We ingest, metabolize, and remake in our imagination and even in new speculative reel narratives, as seen in films by Robert Rodriguez and Alex Rivera. When Princess Leia appears with her famous "cinnamon bun" hairstyle, we recognize this as the style of Mexican women revolutionaries, or *soldaderas*, who fought in Pancho Villa's armies during the Revolution.

And as the *Star Wars* trilogy moves into its prequels and we learn that Bail Organa is Leia's adoptive father, Latinxs respin this into

possible larger worlds: are the Alderaanians brown like Jimmy Smits? Is Alderaan potentially a planet of Latinx peoples?

We also see this in its most decrepit form when Lucas lazily appropriates from stereotypes of Caribbean culture in creating Jar Jar Binks of the Gungans race in *The Phantom Menace*. He is a character with out-of-control dreadlocks, and he speaks trun-

Bail Organa (played by Jimmy Smits) in *Star Wars: Rogue One* (2016)

cated, patois English. He's the black Sambo. He's the bumbling buffoon. This is more than lazy; it's dangerous because Lucas takes filmgoers back to those racist reel reconstructions in *Birth of a Nation* that we discussed earlier in the book.

Lucas is not alone here. Take some recent fantasy films that also reconstruct mythical pasts—all while continuing the brownface Hollywood tradition. For example, Ridley Scott cast *Exodus* (2014) with a panoply of white actors to play Old Testament North Africans, Egyptians, and Jews. Scott chooses blue-eyed Anglo-European actors such as Joel Edgerton (as Ramses II) and Sigourney Weaver (his mother, Tuya) and put them in brownface as ancient Egyptians. Scott's Moses (Christian Bale) experiences his rebirth from Egyptian to warrior Jew *through* brownness. This happens twice: first when he's exiled into the desert, where he survives for months all while the sun and dirt tan him a deep brown, and then when he is mysteriously buried in mud up to his eyes, nose, and mouth and hears the voice of God (anthropomorphized as a young boy). Both are hinge moments in a kind of *Batman* emplotment whereby Moses rebuilds himself into an über-warrior who saves and then leads to the promise land four hundred thousand of the enslaved and disenfranchised. Indeed, Bale's Moses is cut from the same cloth as Charlton Heston's Moses in *The Ten Commandments*: as an Egyptian he's literally squeaky clean, and upon his return to his Jewish roots he becomes brown and dirty while enslaved to work in the mud pits. Even once the dirt washes off, Heston's Moses is browner, tanner.

(Notably, when Ridley Scott does cast actors of color, they are as faithful sidekicks, as with the Roman historical epic, *Gladiator*, where Djimon Hounsou is the sidekick character, Juba, to Russell Crowe's Maximus; the only person of color he cast as a protagonist of a film was Denzel Washington in *American Gangster*. His track record with women protagonists is better: *Alien*, *Thelma and Louise*, and *GI Jane*, for instance.)

Pachucos in Space

While on the topic of Ridley Scott, we applaud his casting of Edward James Olmos as Eduardo Gaff in the groundbreaking sci-fi movie *Blade Runner* (1982). Scott's spectacularly conceived story world includes this wise Latinx figure, whose sartorial wear and mannerisms

Eduardo Gaff (played by Edward James Olmos) in *Blade Runner* (1982)

are through and through pachuco. It's Olmos as a zoot-suiter of the future (recall Luis Valdez's *Zoot Suit* was released in 1981).

With Olmos as the pachuco Gaff, Scott's asking audiences to bridge future and past story worlds: *Blade Runner* with *Zoot Suit*. And Scott and the creators think to invest this Latinx character with smarts and even with the ethical compass to the story world as a whole. He tells Deckerd (Harrison Ford), "It's too bad [Rachel] won't live. But then again, who does?" An aged Gaff makes a brief appearance in Denis Villeneuve's *Blade Runner 2049* (2017). However, here the narrative is most interested in Ryan Gosling: he ends up the one who discovers empathy and, with this, an ethics; he's the one invested in the end with smarts and ethical worldview, sweeping our pachuco (and race and ethnicity generally) into the mise-en-scène shadows.

In the reboot of 1970s sci-fi show *Battlestar Galactica*, Edward James Olmos and outer planetary Latinxs do get their day. As Admiral William Adama he's portrayed as a great rhetor, strategist, leader of the people, and savior of a new generation of existence, the human-cylon Hera.

We learn from the prequel, Ronald D. Moore's *Caprica* (2010–2011), that Adama is a Tauron (coded as Latinx) who ultimately settles his lost tribe on the planet that will be known as Earth. In *Caprica* we learn of the interplanetary racism and bigotry endured by refugees,

coded as Taurons, such as the
Adamas. They are called stinking
dirt eaters by the Anglo-coded
Capricans. The phenotype of the
Taurons with *Caprica* is Esai
Morales as father Joseph Adama.
In *Battlestar* with Olmos as the
grown-up son, William Adama
disrupts preconceptions of Latinos by the use of code-switching,
especially in *Caprica*, where Morales and other Taurons glide
between English, Hebrew, and
Spanish words. *Battlestar Ga-*

William Adama (played by Edward James
Olmos) in *Battlestar Galactica* (season 3,
episode 8, 2006)

lactica and *Caprica* are remarkably innovative. They build into their
story-worlds enough Latinx signposts (especially in the *Caprica*) to
direct audiences to create palimpsests between the Taurons and today's Latinxs. These films also include interventions of characters and
whole communities played by Latinos. While *Star Trek* in all its iterations emphasizes diversity, *Battlestar* and *Caprica* feature prominent
Latinx actors *and* deep allegorical codings of Latinxs that make them
innovative and relevant.

Mixed-Race Futures

Ridley Scott's Gaff is Latinx, and the *Blade Runner* story line also
identifies him as Asian. He's mixed race—and this in the early 1980s,
when few characters were written as such. In the twenty-first century, we see more mixed Latinx characterizations. On prime-time TV,
for example, Evan Katz's *The Event* (2010–2011) featured a blatino
(Afro-Latino Cuban) U.S. president; Elias Martinez (played by non-
blatino actor Blair Underwood) ends up running an administration
that decimates other galactic aliens living among humans *as* humans.
In episode 15, "Face Off," when President Martinez gives the green
light to blow up the aliens, TV audiences overlay these subjects with
the treatment of undocumented Latinxs today. That Clifton Collins Jr.
(grandson of actor Pedro Gonzalez Gonzalez) plays Thomas, one of
the leaders of the aliens, solidifies the link audiences make between

Latinxs in Reel Speculative Spaces

the show's otherworld aliens and those Latinxs deemed "illegal aliens" in real life. Incidentally, Pedro's brother, José Gonzales-Gonzales, appeared as one of the first Latinxs to have a speaking role in a science fiction film (*Kronos*, 1957).

Latinxs as Monstrous Aliens to White Saviors

Latinxs have been and continue to be pejoratively identified as *illegal aliens*. In Barry Sonnenfeld's *Men in Black* (1997). Sonnenfeld chooses to include a prologue of sorts to the film that portrays an Anglo coyote (Jon Gries) transporting undocumented Latinxs across the border into the United States. After they are stopped by a racist Anglo border patroller, Agent K (Tommy Lee Jones) speaks fluent Spanish to the group of Latinxs welcoming them to the United States. Sonnenfeld turns the tables on a long history of Latinx stereotypes in one fell swoop. The more slovenly looking of the Latinxs, José (Sergio Calderon), wearing a poncho, doesn't understand Spanish. This is how Agent K identifies the alien (from space) as *not an alien* (undocumented Latinx).

When Latinxs are reconstructed in the speculative (sci-fi, fantasy, horror) storytelling genres, it's usually as transmogrifying monstrous alien others. In many ways, this *is* how some creators of reel

Latinx border crossers, including José (played by Sergio Calderon), next to Agent K (played by Tommy Lee Jones) in *Men in Black* (1997)

Latinxs see *real* Latinxs in the United States: as vilified, sexualized, alienated (in the sense of being turned into aliens), or some creative and new method for combining those tropes. Reconstructed as a villain, a *sucia*, a bad hombre, or something monstrous is perfidious and deliberate. Add to these reel reconstructions all of the ways Latinxs are reconstructed as sexual objects, as we discussed above, and it's no surprise that there's a tradition of reconstructing Latinxs as *fearful* aliens and monsters.

The monstrous Other doesn't last long, however. The formula for the sci-fi narrative is that a white-savior figure appears to subdue and decimate the monstrous (Latin for "outrageously wrong")—and even experience a kind of Christological rebirth. John McTiernan's film *Predator* (1987) is paradigmatic. It features the protagonist, Dutch (Arnold Schwarzenegger), who reverses his fate and becomes the hunter of the alien predator (somewhere in a South American jungle) after he submerges himself in brown mud and lets out a barbaric yawp. The story establishes this at the moment when Dutch outwits the alien—its perception system can't register Dutch's body heat because he's caked in mud. And it's the mo-

Anna (played by Elpidia Carrillo) in *Predator* (1987)

ment of his rebirth, through the brown mud—a mud that ultimately saves him and the lone Latina warrior, Anna (Elpidia Carrillo), from the alien. That is, he's reborn in and across the brown other. We see the same narrative in the sequel, Nimród Antal's *Predators* (2010), that features Royce (Adrian Brody) as the white savior who outlasts all the characters of color, including Cuchillo (Danny Trejo), and conquers the alien.

Whether it be outer space, aliens in South American jungles, or fantastically imagined Western frontiers, the white-savior myth remains all pervasive. In *Cowboys and Aliens* (2011) Jon Favreau offers a creative mash-up of science fiction with the Western. It also features a few Latinxs: the slovenly bandit Bronc (Julio Cedillo), who fumbles the box of matches needed to dynamite the alien space ship.

Bronc (played by Julio Cedillo) in *Cowboys and Aliens* (2011)

Cowboys and Aliens also includes other characters of color, such as the wild bandit Nat Colorado (Salteaux First Nations' Native actor Adam Beach) and the saloon "maid" María (Ana de la Reguera). However, the Latinx Bronc and the indigenous Others all play as secondary and disposable characters to the white protagonist, Jake Lonergan (Daniel Craig), who saves the cowboys and Indians—along with the entire galaxy—from a technologically advanced, invading alien nation. As is pro forma, the white guy's ingenuity is given sharp focus *only after* he's reborn through brownness. In this instance, he's reborn after a vision-quest ceremony. And with this vision-questing ceremony, we see how Favreau is doubly bound to two genres that have historically resisted incorporating brown people as complex, heroic, and relevant characters. Rather than upset those limiting genre traditions, Favreau upholds them and adds the technological advancements of special effects.

Recently, there was a cowboy–sci-fi mash-up that radically innovated this tried and tired formula. HBO's *Westworld* (2017–) was all

Hector Escatón (played by Rodrigo Santoro) in *Westworld* (season 1, episode 1, 2017)

about the revolt of the robots (from *roboti*, which derives from the Old Church Slavonic *rabota*, or servitude), many of which are ethnically and racially identified. Indeed, the robot revolt is against their white British master, apotheosized by Anthony Hopkins in his role as Dr. Robert Ford. While it's African American prostitute turned revolutionary Maeve Millay (Thandie Newton) who leads the revolution, Latinxs feature in prominent roles in the robot revolution—Clifton Collins Jr. as the gunslinging Latinx outlaw robot Lawrence, and Rodrigo Santoro as Latinx cowboy womanizer robot Hector Escatón, who wakes to his servitude and speciesism.

With James Gunn's runaway hits *Guardians of the Galaxy* (2014) and *Guardians of the Galaxy Vol. 2* (2017), not only do we encounter the tired Anglo-savior myth, with Chris Pratt as Peter Quill/Star Lord stepping in at the end to save the galaxy, but anything Latinx about the actors and actresses is lost. The movie features ambiguously racially marked Vin Diesel, but here as a tree creature with few words and lots of branches. (Notably, in comic-book creator Edgardo Miranda-Rodriguez's revision of Groot, he anchors his ancestry in the Ceiba tree as a symbolic gesture toward his Puerto Rican Taino indigenous roots.) It stars a recognizable Benicio del Toro as the Collector, but he's been given a bleach-blonde-hair makeover. And it features Zoe Saldana as one of the leads, but she's in greenface, literally. *Guardians of the Galaxy* (2014) ends with Saldana as Gamora, standing behind the Anglo Quill, stating "We'll follow your lead, Star Lord."

We mentioned already several times Cameron's *Avatar* and the rebirth of the white savior in and through a mystically identified indigenous (alien) Other. This same mystical rebirth narrative formula weaves its way through many other sci-fi films, and to an even more exaggerated degree. *The Fountain* (2006) takes the white-savior myth to another level altogether. Darren Aronofsky uses the sci-fi storytelling envelope and adds a heavy dose of spiritualism to literally transmute white into brown across huge expanses of time and space. Hugh Jackman plays three different protagonists: a modern-day oncologist, Tommy; a superhumanly fit Spanish conquistador, Tomas Creo, who is attacked by a marauding Mayan high priest covered in tattoos and wielding a dagger; and a Buddhist-like figure, Tom, who inhabits an outer-galactic biosphere.

Tomas Creo (played by Hugh Jackman) in *The Fountain* (2006)

At the film's close, Tommy, Tomas, and Tom become one as he reaches some sort of nirvanic state. He's seen sitting in the lotus position and enveloped in white light as he ascends into the universe from his New Age biospheric spacecraft. We see something similar in *Cloud Atlas*, based on David Mitchell's novel of the same name. The film takes the same core group of actors and imagines them at various points in time as reincarnated characters. The take on nirvana is reminiscent of *2001: A Space Odyssey*, when Bowman slowly progresses through stages until he dies, shedding his mortal coil to be reborn as the Star Child. In the case of Aronofsky's film, there is the idea of the difference in melanin or phenotype (Jackman doesn't change *that* much) as being superficial and perhaps superfluous in the larger, nirvanic sense of things. It's the equivalent to those who say there are no races, only the *human* race. Until we live in a truly postracial world, this is a destructive idealism.

More recently, the film adaptation of *Annihilation* (2018) reveals what is now becoming a kind of norm—it is a film that falls short in one area of diverse representations while also signaling progress in other areas. The film's premise involves an unknown, extraterrestrial phenomenon known as The Shimmer that has settled over an undisclosed area of the U.S. East Coast. Every team that has been sent into The Shimmer has not returned, except for one—Kane (Oscar Isaac), who is the husband of the protagonist, Lena (Natalie Portman). Kane has returned, changed in substantive ways that remain a mystery throughout. Lena, together with a group of women, including Anya Thorensen (Gina Rodriguez), enter The Shimmer to find some answers. It is stunning to see a kind of action film that features a group of women as a militarized strike team because this doesn't happen in Hollywood (the film blows past the Bechdel Test with ease).

Annihilation features two prominent Latinx actors, Isaac and Rodriguez, yet they are not coded as Latinx in the film. Anya becomes paranoid and is killed two-thirds of the way into the film. The film is also problematic because it takes characters that were Asian in the novel and whitens them with white actresses. Though director Alex Garland claims he did not know of the characters' Asian ancestry (the book is the first of a trilogy, and the characters' race is not denoted until the second book, which Garland claims he did not read), critics still hold the film as yet another example of the trend of whitewashing Asian characters in Hollywood films.

Fishing for Latinxs in Sci-Fi Story Worlds

In the past, finding Latinxs in mainstream sci-fi was a real fishing expedition. We ask, How far do we cast our net in trying to identify

Latinx in the sci-fi, comic-book, fantasy story world universe? Do we identify Sue Storm in *Fantastic Four* (2005) as Latina because she's played by Jessica Alba— albeit a totally blonde Alba?

Is Sue Storm a Latina because Alba can't leave her Latina phenotype off set? Are Benicio del Toro's characters in *Guardians of the Galaxy* and *Star Wars: The Last Jedi* somehow Latinx? What happens in our brains when we know an actor fits a specific

Sue Storm (played by Jessica Alba) in *Fantastic Four* (2005)

identity position in our world yet plays something else on screen? Is this suspension of disbelief again, or are there always traces of the actors; identities in the DNA of the characters they play? Think of Chris Tucker in *The Fifth Element*, with his blond hair and atypical representation of black masculinity. Is DJ Ruby Rhod, famous intergalactic radio host, now a black character?

With the original *Star Trek* TV series, we had to make do with either black, Asian, or Klingon (white actors in blackface) characters. It did, however, give Latinx TV audiences Nichelle Nichols as the smart, badass Uhura and the incomparable Japanese American actor George Takei as Sulu. These two actors portrayed their iconic characters as complex and nuanced, and they avoided stereotypical renditions of black women and Asian men. George Takei, whose character Sulu had achieved captain status on his own ship in *Star Trek VI: The Undiscovered Country* (1991), notably refused to reprise his role in the generational crossover film *Star Trek: Generations* because the film once more showed Sulu in a past moment in time before he was captain. Takei felt that it was a step back, and he turned down the role. *Star Trek: The Undiscovered Country* featured the character Azetbur, the daughter of Klingon chancellor Gorkon. Azetbur was played by Rosanna DeSoto, who also played Latina characters in *Stand and Deliver* and *La Bamba.*

Azetbur (played by Rosanna DeSoto) in *Star Trek VI: The Undiscovered Country* (1991)

DeSoto may be the most prominent Latina to star in a *Star Trek* film or show. As the daughter of such a high-ranking Klingon official, the character becomes a powerful player in deciding whether the Klingon Empire will go to war with the Federation. Azetbur has integrity and is not duplicitous. While the character is not Latina, the Latina playing her is given the opportunity to stay away from simple stereotypes that are associated with either Latinxs or Klingons.

Earlier in this book we mentioned that in *Star Trek Voyager* (1995–2001) B'Elanna Torres (Roxann Dawson) struggles with her mixed-race identity as Klingon and human but that the writing subordinates her Latinidad. Her struggle comes from her Klingon side. In this same show, however, there appears another Latinx character, Commander Chakotay (played by mixed Native and Latinx actor Robert Beltran). In the show, Chakotay is of Native American ancestry, and his people are undergoing another process of relocation, this time to an interstellar reservation of sorts. They get an entire planet, but only momentarily, of course. Still, Beltran looks like the brown-skinned Latinx we rarely see in the *Star Trek* universe who isn't hidden behind heavy layers of makeup or facial prosthetics. The original *Star Trek* TV series also created the notable role of Khan Noonien Singh, played by the inimitable Mexican-born Ricardo Montalbán. But for all of the character's panache and complexity, Khan appeared only once more, albeit much more prominently, in the film *Star Trek II: The Wrath of Khan*.

Something rather monumental happened in 2000 in terms of the conception of Latinxs in science-fiction TV shows. James Cameron cast Jessica Alba as Max Guevara in the show *Dark Angel* (2000–2008). She's not loaded down with heavy markers of Latinidad. Rather, she's identified as part of a multiracial, urban, postapocalyptic new world. The show was set in Seattle in 2019—only a few years from the time of writing this book. Alba as Max is a tomboy bike messenger who works alongside a cadre of ethnic (ambiguous mixes) types. This is a world of draconian rule and surveillance, where the gulf between the haves and have-nots has become more extreme. However, more interestingly, the show is a projection of how ethnic mixtures destabilize notions of purity. It's not about spotting Blacks or Latinxs or Asians—they all look mixed, and this is the dominant demographic for the have-nots. The few Anglo characters shown are either bosses, of military rank, or wealthy. Max's own ethnic background is elided, and instead the viewer is meant to be attracted to her ethnic ambiguity, as shown in her brown skin color and Anglo features—just as we are meant to engage with a world filled with twenty-somethings who are all mixed. Max overcomes her deep angst and sense of isolation as an Other and leads the mutated and cross-species entities known as Transgenics (the ultimate in racial Otherness) to civil rights struggles and gains. After an eight-year run, Cameron ends the series with the episode "Freak Nation" (produced by Renée Echevaría) with Alba, her metahuman brothers and sisters, and the Transgenics in solidarity, demanding civil rights. They all stand in solidarity with Black Panther-like fists of power in the air after Max declares, "We were made in America and we are not going anywhere."

At the end of the day, Max is written as ambiguously Latinx. She is denoted as Latina mostly through her surname, Guevara. Alba, herself, sits right at the intersection of many phenotypic traditions. In the right contexts she might play a white character, or a Latina, for instance. *Dark Angel* is a notable historical point in the portrayal of Latinos in science-fiction TV in the United States. It helped launch Alba's career and may turn out to be an intriguing path opened up for Latinas in speculative fictions to come.

Dark Angel was a hit. It had an eight-season run and shattered simple representations of the Other and people of color on TV. When these sorts of groundbreaking smash hits appear, there is a rush to clone them. Yet prime-time TV didn't want to create more and different iterations of *Dark Angel*. Instead, it went the route of *Humans* and *Orphan Black*, which are less confrontational about their revolutionary message—and certainly don't feature any Latinx characters.

Reel Latinx Superheroes, Wherefore Art Thou?

For the most part, comic-book re-creations don't feature any Latinxs—even when they do appear in their comic-book originals and when the story worlds they recreate are of the present or near-present everyday United States. Joss Whedon's *The Avengers* is certainly science-fiction fantasy, but it has a foot planted in the everyday reality we recognize. Yet when his Avengers save the planet, there are no brown people present in the general population. The same can be said of Zack Snyder's *Man of Steel*—another comic-book film that has one foot firmly planted in today's world but shows only two Latinxs: a gas attendant and a Latina soldier. Actually, the only person of color prominently featured in *Man of Steel* is Laurence Fishburne as Perry White. As for Latinxs, these reconstructions willfully absent our presence. Kenneth Branagh's *Thor* unfolds largely in the fictional town of Agua Puento; Branagh filmed it in Galisteo, New Mexico, a Latinx majority state.

The story is located in a recognizable Southwest region but without Latinxs, and the story's coherence falls apart. Branagh did film some Latinxs (children playing ball) in the town, but he cut them for the final movie we saw in the theater.

You'd think we'd at least be represented in the film re-creations of the *X-Men* comics—a comic-book series born of the advances in our civil rights struggles. In Singer's first installment, *X-Men* (2000), the story establishes a sort of palimpsest whereby mutants are to be read as an allegory for today's racial Others and specifically as Latinxs, the group that moves "among us" and that threatens the "American way of life," as declared by the conservative Senator Robert Kelley at the beginning of the film. We are reminded of the phrase "undocumented among us"—the rhetoric of today's white-nationalist, alt-right movement, the rhetoric that constantly bemoans the fantasy of "wanting their country back" or "a return to better times." It's the same rhetoric of *The Clansman* and *The Birth of a Nation*.

The fact is, in all the DC and Marvel film re-creations, Latinxs are either invisible or hard to find. In *X-Men* there's a rather oblique reference to *lucha libre* when the referee of a fight introduces with great hyperbole Logan's character as "King of the Cage: Wolverine." In Singer's *X-Men 2* (2003) Latinxs appear as janitors; Singer chose to cut completely screen time given to the Latina mutant Angel Salvadore. When director Brett Ratner takes over the helm of the franchise, how-

Laura X-23 (played by Dafne Keen) in *Logan* (2017)

ever, things improve somewhat. In his *X-Men: Last Stand* (2006), some screen time is given over to Dania Ramirez as the Latina mutant Callisto, who is quickly made disposable.

Logan is arguably the best example of Latinxs in an *X-Men* film. While we have a stereotypical representation of the Latinx gangbangers at the film's opening, the remaining representations of Latinos are nuanced, complex, and not always idealized. *Logan* embraces the Latinx experience that has been sorely lacking in the *X-Men* franchise, and audiences are rewarded for it. The center of the film concerns a deteriorating Charles Xavier, aka Professor X (Patrick Stewart), Logan (Hugh Jackman), and his heretofore unknown daughter, Laura (newcomer Dafne Keen, who is of Spanish heritage).

Logan and Professor X have been hiding near the Mexican border when a woman named Gabriela (Elizabeth Rodriguez) offers to pay Logan to drive her and Laura to the northern U.S.-Canada border and ostensible safety. Laura has been a part of a clandestine experiment in Mexico that has manipulated and used mutant DNA to create children. Thus, unbeknownst to Logan, Laura shares his extraordinary healing ability because she is his daughter. The film is a process of relationship building and growing trust between the two of them, which is made more poignant because they speak different languages since Laura is culturally Mexican. Spanish is heard throughout the film, and Latinx identity at least is a substantial notion as well. Even this cannot be said of previous *X-Men* films. The film was a critical and box-office success, and currently has a 93 percent Certified Fresh rating on Rotten Tomatoes with an audience score of 90 percent. *Logan* is a clear example that blockbuster films with significant characters and signifiers of Latinidad can be successful by typical film-industry standards.

Pitof's *Catwoman* (2004) received howls from the critics. The CGI effects are really not good. But it's one of few comic-book films that gives some decent airtime to Latinxs. Not only is Halle Berry as Patience Phillips given a racial ambiguity that can be read as hispanophone Latina (Puerto Rican or Dominican), but Pitof casts Benjamin Bratt as the detective and love interest. The story world doesn't ignore the presence of Latinxs—an increasingly urban population. The hinge moment of the film and when she comes into her full awareness of her new powers comes when Berry and Bratt play basketball with a crowd of Latinx and African American kids cheering them on. We see *Catwoman* as both a setback for Latinxs and a breakthrough. Though it's easy to shake your head at this, I'm glad that these moments happen— these opportunities to include Latinxs as a part of the superhero business that is booming worldwide.

We have to discuss Christopher Nolan's *Batman* trilogy, especially *The Dark Knight Rises*. Nolan missed an opportunity to cast a Latinx in the role of Bane, arguably the most important, smart, and sophisticated Latinx supervillain in the DC universe. He chose instead to cast British actor Tom Hardy. But had he cast, say, Javier Bardem as the villain, we might be discussing why a Latinx had to be cast as the villain. Here we might nuance the simple formulation: cast a white actor as prominent bad guy results in overlooking Latinx actors; cast a Latino as prominent bad guy poses the question, why are Latinos always bad guys? We still wonder, based on his Oscar-winning turn as the evil Anton Chiggur in *No Country for Old Men*, how great Javier Bardem could have been as Bane.

The introduction of Peter Parker (played by British actor Tom Holland) into the Marvel Cinematic Universe, while a seeming necessary move because he is the original Spider-Man, ignores the popularity and contributions of Miles Morales, who has donned the Spider-Man mantle post–Peter Parker. In *Spider-Man: Homecoming* (2017), there are no Latinx characters, though Peter's best friend and sidekick, Ned (Jacob Batalon, Hawaiian-born Filipino), is Asian. Despite this, the computer-animated feature film *Spider-Man: Into the Spider-Verse* (2018) is Miles Morales's big screen debut and is the first instance of a blatino superhero character represented in a feature film. Again, given that Latinxs are visibly present in the DC and Marvel comic-book universes, you'd think this would work its way into the cinematic universes. It doesn't. Latinxs are lost in the translation and adaptation.

Televisual Latinx Superheroes

With the exception of a few shows such as *Smallville* and *Gotham* (2014–) that either absent Latinxs altogether or feature only a few, TV seems to be doing a slightly better job with reconstructing our real presence in superhero sci-fi worlds. Let's take a long-running TV show such as *Smallville* (2001–2011). We don't fault it for featuring Clark Kent as a teen, then young adult, fighting for the greater good and so on. However, within its ten-year run and 218 episodes, only a few Latinxs have been cast. For example, Arcata (Andrea Rojas) works a desk job at the *Daily Planet* by day and is the Angel of Vengeance (Denise Quiñones, former Miss Puerto Rico 2001) by night. Arcata occasionally peppers her English with one-liners such as "Let it go, comprende" (see season 5, episode 13, "Vengeance"). And Jaime Reyes turns into the Blue Beetle. He doesn't sprinkle his phrases with

Cisco "Vibe" Ramone (played by Carlos Valdes) in *The Flash* (season 3, episode 11, 2016)

Spanishisms, but he does sport a T-shirt with "El Paso" on it (see season 10, episode 18, "Booster").

CW's TV show *The Flash* features an Anglo superhero, Barry Allen, but here at least Cisco Ramon (Carlos Valdes) is portrayed as a tech and math genius. In the comic-book world, Cisco becomes the superhero, Vibe, and is cast against the grain of the stereotype. He's a mathematical whiz, which we find to be refreshing. However, his role seems to be to clean up all the messes in which Barry Allen (Grant Gustin) finds himself. A high-tech-savvy Latinx Cisco remains the brown janitor to the story's white savior of Central City—a city itself oddly devoid of Latinxs. He's the Joe Dominguez to Barry Allen's Nash Bridges. It makes sense. What would be truly groundbreaking would be to have Barry Allen played by a Latinx (a story change would be that his father was white but his mother was Latina) and have the sidekick role played by the white actor.

Tim Kring's *Heroes* (NBC 2006–2010) is not based on a comic book, but it is a comic-book TV show. It features a contemporary United States filled to the brim with metahumans that can see the future, regenerate, and jump space/time continua. Several such superheroes are Latinxs, including the twins Maya (played by Dominican American Dania Ramirez) and Alejandro Herrera (played by Puerto Rican American Shalom Ortiz). In their escape from their native Dominican Republic, they are depicted crossing borders (Guatemala to Mexico and Mexico to the United States), along the way learning how to control their superhero powers: Maya's lethal poisoning of others when stressed and her brother's ability to deactivate her power (see episodes 1–11, 2007–2008). It's a superhero show with intriguing, nuanced representations of Latinxs.

The real innovations are happening in TV's digital spaces, as with webisodes tied to prime-time TV shows such as *Agents of S.H.I.E.L.D.*

Elena "Yo-Yo" Rodriguez (played by Natalia Cordova-Buckley) in *Agents of S.H.I.E.L.D* (season 3, episode 11, 2017)

In that show (season 3, episode 11, "Bouncing Back"), Joss Whedon introduces viewers to the Latina superhero character Elena "Yo-Yo" Rodriguez (played by Natalia Cordova-Buckley).

Yo-Yo (also known in the print comic as Slingshot) is street smart, independent, and a metahuman; she can move at super speeds in the duration of one heartbeat. But it's what happens at the webisode margins that's of greater interest. In the six webisodes (three to five minutes long each) attached to the TV show, she becomes the protagonist of her own narrative. She's smart and hyperaware of the reel stereotypical reconstructions of real Latinxs. For instance, in the first webisode, "Vendetta," after Coulson tells her that by signing on as an agent of SHIELD she can't go directly after Ramon, the thug who killed her cousin, she remarks, "I thought America was all about freedom. When I use my powers, it should be my choice." In a remarkable moment for mainstream writing of Latinas, she expresses concern that America (SHIELD agency as a kind of microcosm and stand-in for the United States) limits her own agency.

It's no secret that we should all desire to see Latinxs in unexpected reel roles. These should be unexpected in our own reality because Latinxs run the gamut of talents and abilities in our society today. It's just that reel reconstructions perpetuate the fallacy that Latinxs fall only within narrow characterizations or abilities.

Zombies and More

Comic-book, fantasy, and sci-fi genres have increasingly moved from margins to centers, all while leaving Latinxs in the proverbial dust. We see this also with recent zombie and vampire/werewolf narrative trends. Latinxs are depicted either directly as Others or through allegorical means. Latinxs appear more directly and refreshingly as Others. There's a scene in the comic-book film adaptation *World War Z* (2013) where desperate hordes of zombies clamber over giant walls that the "healthy" humans (most clearly represented by the savior, Brad Pitt as Gerry) built around Jerusalem. Indeed, the first humans that we see turn into zombies are Latinxs—a Latinx family that helps save the Anglos, Gerry and his wife, Karin. The wall brings to mind the wall along the U.S.-Mexico border and Latinxs crossing into the United States. Jerusalem brings to mind Palestinians, walled off in the "occupied territories." It all also reads like an allegory of today's use of "the wall" as a phrase/image/idea to fan xenophobia—the alt-right nationalist fantasy that somehow building a wall at the U.S. southern border will keep out the unwanted hordes of brown people.

In contrast with films like *World War Z*, which create allegories where Latinxs are present as the marauding hordes trying to cross borders established by "healthy" Anglos, in Javier Hernandez's comic book and Brian Cox's film re-creation of *El muerto* (2007) not only does an actual Latinx play the role of protagonist (Wilmer Valderama), but the story's characters cross U.S.-Mexico borders and take audiences deep into precolonial and colonial history and mythology.

While crossing into the United States, Juan Diego experiences a shamanistic awakening (by way of the "Indio Viejo" character, played by Billy Drago) that leads to the marking of the god Tezcatlipoca, god of sacrifice, on Diego's hand. Later, when Diego is twenty-one, he feels the call of the underworld—of the god of death, Mictlantecuhtli, and goes to a Day of the Dead festival dressed as an undead Mariachi with a skeletal look. He crashes on the way to the festival and awakens in the Aztec afterlife of Mictlan, where he's sacrificed to Tezcatlipoca. He's restored to the earthly world only to battle the forces of Tezcatlipoca, who seeks to destroy his love interest, Maria (Angie Cepeda).

Prime-Time Vampires

Vampire Diaries features Latino actor Michael Anthony Trevino as Tyler Lockwood, a leather-wearing bad boy. As is typical of the vampire/werewolf genre, the brown Others are typically werewolves—and the vampires are Anglo aristocrats. (We see this also in *Twilight*, with phenotypically brown actors such as Taylor Lautner playing the werewolves.)

AMC's *The Walking Dead* (2010–) and SyFy's *Z Nation* (2014–) at once offer horrortainment as well as the Latinx threat narrative all dressed up in zombie attire. In *Walking Dead's* "Vatos" (season 1, episode 4) the Anglo-savior character, Rick Grimes (Brit actor Andrew Lincoln), and his multiculti ragtag team encounter some *vatos locos* in a postapocalyptic Atlanta. Juan Pareja (as Morales) and Noel Gugliemi (as Felipe) exaggerate Chicanx slang and sartorial wear to be sure the audience gets that they are Latinx gangbangers.

In a recent episode of *Z Nation* (season 2, episode 15), Gina Gershwin appears in brownface as a Latina bruja (and leader of a pack of *calavera*-painted, machete-wielding Anglos) who imitates the stereotypical speech intonation of an East L.A. chola. In both cases, it's the white-savior-led erasure (left behind or annihilation) of Latinxs

Morales (played by Juan Pareja) and Felipe (played by Noel Gugliemi) in *Walking Dead* (season 1, episode 4, 2010)

that propels the narrative forward. If we consider our zombietainment options, then Rodriguez's imaginary *is* clearing a new, decolonial productive reel Latinx space.

The Walking Dead is a zombie TV show that occasionally surprises. It features the typical Anglo-savior myth, to be sure. Anglo cop Rick Grimes becomes part of a ragtag group of survivors just outside Atlanta. However, the creators of the show are aware of race and racism. In one episode the white Aryan, Merle "Dixon," calls a Latinx character a "Taco Bender." Grimes tries to create solidarity by declaring that in a world filled with zombies there's no race, only dark meat and white meat. (See the episode titled "Guts.") And in another episode, "Vatos," Grimes and his crew come into contact with a Latino cholo gang in Atlanta. The Latinos punctuate their sentences with *carnal, puto, vato, ese*. They wear the cholo bandana and Pendleton shirt look, and the leader, Guillermo, wears all the Catholic accouterment possible. Their hideout against the zombies is a chop shop. It's the *abuelita* who calms down the gang to prevent them from shooting Rick and his crew. But the show does something interesting: it turns all these stereotypes on their heads. As it turns out, the violence of the Latinx gang was a performance aimed to protect a more complex and intergenerational Latinx community; the gang was performing the bad-boy cholo in order to keep others away from the food and medicine they had stored for their elders.

Zombie narratives allow for some intriguing inversions of the ways in which identity groups tend to work in the United States. When Grimes refers to white and dark meat, he is essentially articulating the idealistic canard, "there is only one race: the human race." Yet in that instance he's exactly right. Speculative writers often unite humanity by creating a warlike extraterrestrial that wants to conquer the planet. Suddenly no one really cares whether you have an accent or a certain amount of melanin. *The Walking Dead* operates in this fashion—until late in the series, the zombies almost take a backseat to the tribalism that comes to the fore, one that is not based on heritage or race but typically on some other unifying characteristic of identity.

Let's end this reflection by celebrating zombies and more in the hands of Latinx re-creators. Within digital spaces there's the twelve-web-episode series *Brujos*—broadcast by Open TV, an online platform "for queer and intersectional television." Its mash-up of telenovela and sitcom formula, along with some *brujería*, provide the narrative envelope for the show to address racism, homophobia, and (straight, white male) colonization. And there's the long tradition of the zombie in reel Mexican reconstructions. El Santo is constantly at battle with the undead and other supernatural creatures in *Santo contra los zombies* (1962) and *Santo contra los asesinos de otros mundos* (1973), with the scandalously infamous Sasha Montenegro, as well as *Santo y la venganza de La Llorona* (1974). Blue Demon is another masked luchador superhero who is pitted against these foes. The supernatural and superstition loom large in many Latin American cultures and thus in Latinx communities in the United States.

Latinxs Strike Back

Latinx film directors like Robert Rodriguez and Alex Rivera have used the sci-fi and horror narrative mold to strike back. For instance, we see in *Sleep Dealer* (2008) how global capitalists use advances in technology to exploit Mexican braceros, forcing them to work longer hours and not have to cross the border and sully the United States.

Rivera constructs a film that portrays how the automatized Latinx borderland subject represents the reality of a brown-body labor force that is made to see itself as a machine. Not only does Rivera use the sci-fi format to present a political critique of the exploitation of Latinxs—and also the United States' control over water rights that

Memo Cruz (played by Luis Fernando Peña) in *Sleep Dealer* (2008)

determine the fates of families in Mexico—but leaves the audience with some hope for humanity. Memo Cruz's (Luis Fernando Peña) nemesis, Rudy Ramirez (Jacob Vargas), uses drone technology to blow up a corporate controlled dam (Del Rio Water) to give water back to the Mexican people. Here Rivera creates a compelling story of the near future that, now ten years later, seems eerily prescient. The emphasis on drones that roam with the go-ahead to shoot to kill, the militarization and closing off of the U.S.-Mexico border, the emphasis on reality TV, and the deportation of "undesirables" while importing their mechanized labor are spot on. He uses the sci-fi envelope to create a compelling narrative about the condition of being an exploitable Mexican. He also presents to the world the fact that Latinx film directors can also choose to create sci-fi narratives that put Latinx experiences and subjectivities front and center.

Let's not forget Robert Rodriguez's *The Faculty* (1998) and *Planet Terror* (2007). They straddle several genres, including science fiction and horror. But *Planet Terror* presents more forcefully an expression of Latinidad. Cherry (Rose McGowan) leads the people to the Promised Land—Tulum, Mexico—with an infant strapped to her back—symbolizing a new generation of Latinxs that's the product

El Wray (played by Freddy Rodriguez) in *Planet Terror* (2007)

both of woman warrior Cherry and superhero badass El Wray (Freddy Rodriguez).

Elsewhere, Christopher talks about this as a "post post-Latinidad" that sidesteps "overt markers of Latinidad and instead uses a handful of decisive signs of Latinidad in specific moments in his cinematic storyworlds." Rodriguez can do this and trouble the long history of reel reconstructions of Latinxs because he knows his film history and he chooses to sidestep explicit signposts of Latinidad. He is subtler, until at the end he has all the survivors cross the U.S.-Mexico border *in a southern direction*. Tulum is the place of refuge, representing a return to a symbolic foundation of Latinidad. Rodriguez uses the sci-fi and exploitation formats in making *Planet Terror* to radically complicate the Latinx experience and identity.

Robert Rodriguez's *Machete Kills* (2013) is a mash-up that includes as one of its ingredients the sci-fi genre. It alludes to films such as Lewis Gilbert's 1979 *Moonraker*; Marko Zaror plays a Latinofied bodyguard akin to Jaws, and Mel Gibson as Luther Voz, a Hugo Drax. With the inclusion of a Landspeeder it also alludes to George Lucas's 1977 *Star Wars*. And Machete rides a nuclear bomb much like Major T. J. "King" Kong in Stanley Kubrick's *Dr. Strangelove* (1964). Rodriguez's trailer for the forthcoming sequel, *Machete in Space*, has him wielding a lightsaber. Elsewhere Christopher calls this "intertextploitation": the idea that he exploits intertextual moments from other films, and especially his own, for particular aesthetic designs, that is, *Planet Terror* and *From Dusk till Dawn*.

We Want Our Wakanda!

With the unqualified success of the film *Black Panther* (2018), we have an epic heroic story from the comic-book universe that delivers the nuance of community and brings us complex heroes and complex villains. Everything about the film, from its design to its casting, evinces a respect for African heritage and culture. Its engagement with black masculinities and feminisms while acknowledging the effects of colonialism, isolationism, white supremacy, and black militant ideologies is breathtaking. We want that for Latinx audiences, and Latinx audiences deserve such a film. We want our Wakanda and a world where

Latinx bodies and minds are the prime movers of a filmic story world. We want our Black Panther for Latinx filmgoing audiences. We hope *Black Panther* has set off seismic shifts in the film and TV industry in how they view difference and diversity. *Black Panther*, now the most financially successful superhero film in U.S. history, has made what was once thought impossible now very probable.

Coda

IT'S A LATINX WRAP

Straightjackets to the Mainstream Imaginary

As we finish this book, Steven Spielberg's much-hyped *Ready Player One* (2018) just hit theaters. It's another *Avatar* moment in reel Latinx film history—and maybe worse. That is, technically Spielberg takes film entertainment to a new level. For the first time, there's a seamless integration of CGI otherworlds with the realism of everyday life. There are no glitches in the postproduction digital effects that might have one hesitate as we move back and forth between the Oasis and 2044 of Columbus, Ohio. However, we wonder whether Spielberg and his creative team (and here we include the author, Ernest Cline, of the like-titled book) has ever stepped outside their doors—or videogame consoles. We've already thrown our hands up at how many times we go to see a blockbuster film and it's always a straight, white male protagonist. The white savior, Wade Watts, and his avatar Parzival (Percival was one of the legendary knights at King Arthur's round table) save the day.

We're not going to get upset again about this. What's unbelievable to us is that in 2018 we have a film that's set in 2044 where there are *no* Latinxs. Chris Rock criticized the white Oscars, telling his audience that you have to go out of your way *not to see a brown person in L.A.* It's the same nationally. So, while Spielberg includes the token African American and Asian sidekick characters, there are no Latinxs to be found—not even in the background shots.

When demographers predict that Latinxs will be *the majority* in the United States in 2065, this is yet again a case of a creator willfully erasing through their reel reconstructions the *real* presence of Latinxs. Within the first couple of minutes we learn from the voice-over (the narrator and protagonist Wade Watts) that in the Oasis the only limits one has is the imagination. And so, we have yet another $175 million film that will likely entertain millions of people that not only lacks imagination but that willfully ignores the reality from which it extrapolates.

Latinx Bechdel Test

We end with a discussion of some of the Latinx films and TV shows that have at least two named Latinx characters who have at least one conversation that is not about an Anglo. The reel narratives that are most interesting in terms of Latinx are happening in the streaming and digital margins. We talked earlier about *Brujos.* There are others, including one of our favorites, those nine-minute or so episodes of *East Willy B* (2011–) on YouTube; they have to be some of the best Latinx reel reconstructions done yet. And, with Netflix's *One Day at a Time* (recently canceled despite being renewed for a third season, thanks to its huge Latinx audience following and the watchful eye of National Hispanic Media Coalition), we can stream a narrative (shaped in the traditional sitcom, multicamera way) with a complex range of Latinidad: *mamá* as divorced vet who suffers from PTSD, an out queer daughter, a first-gen *abuela* from Cuba (Peter Pan generation). In this Latinx-revamped *One Day at a Time* we also see that behind the camera all of the show's directors have been people of color, women, or both. These are the shows that pass the Latinx Bechdel Test. And we love them.

Here is our plug for the arts and humanities as it pertains to Latinx students who come from Latinx households who would like to pursue careers in teaching, in writing, in filmmaking, in creating art. Students who get into the halls of institutions of higher education—if they remained unconvinced that they should stay home and get a job—are often warned that there is no future in these arts and humanities endeavors. So they get worried and change their majors to business or something in the sciences. We want to see students envision pathways to achieve their dreams. We *want* them to be writers for TV or to be filmmakers. Internship pipelines need to be created for Latinx directors and screenwriters, for artists and actors. And we as critics need to continue to draw critical attention to #ReelSoWhite. This is how we will diversify the filmmaking and TV business. If we don't continue to act in all the ways we can, then we'll be waiting a long time for Hollywood showmen (and they are men) to make these necessary changes.

Reel and Real Latinxs Today and Tomorrow

As we've begun to show in this brief but expansive snapshot, real Latinxs have been and continue to be reconstructed as *reel* Latinxs in mainstream film and TV—and usually not to the degree of presence and complexity we would expect. This speaks to the way mainstream creators see and don't see real, living, breathing Latinxs today.

Much work must be done at the level of politics, policy and law making, education, and deep within socioeconomic structures. Without systemic change, Latinxs will continue to be tragically underrepresented in college and will be cornered in ways that disallow the full realization of their creative and intellectual potentialities. And the abundant presence of Latinxs in pop culture today is relative. As we already mentioned in the beginning of our book, Latinxs make up 18 percent of the population but exist in less than 3 percent of mainstream cultural phenomena. And, as we've examined herein, plenty of that 2 percent is actively denigrative.

This said, the other thread running through this book is that Latinxs are not passive, absorptive sponges of these reel reconstructions. And, with access to digital media and internet mechanisms of distribution to increase audiences, we've seen some extraordinary examples of how televisual and film formats can be used to tell a multiplicity of Latinx stories and to represent characters that reflect the myriad ways that we exist in the world. With this in mind, we're optimistic for a better reel tomorrow.

FURTHER READINGS AND VIEWINGS

Preface

CHiPs. New York: NBC, 1977–1983.

Miller, Julie. "How Chris Rock Addressed the #OscarsSoWhite Controversy in His Oscars Monologue." *Vanity Fair*, February 28, 2016. https://www.vanityfair.com/hollywood /2016/02/chris-rock-oscars-monologue-oscarssowhite.

Obolor, Suzanne. *Ethnic Labels, Latino Lives: Identity and the Politics of (Re)Presentation in the United States*. Minneapolis: University of Minnesota Press, 1995.

One Day at a Time. Los Angeles: Netflix, 2017–2019.

Rodríguez, Richard T. "X Marks the Spot." *Cultural Dynamics* 29, no. 3 (2017): 202–13. Print.

Salinas, Cristobal, Jr., and Adele Lozano. "Mapping and Recontexualizing the Evolution of the Term *Latinx*: An Environmental Scanning in Higher Education." *Journal of Latinos and Education* (2017). https://doi.org/10.1080/15348431.2017.1390464.

Sundstrom, Ronald R. *The Browning of America and the Evasion of Social Justice*. Albany, NY: SUNY Press, 2008.

Unkrich, Lee, and Adrian Molina, screenplay. *Coco*. Emeryville, Calif.: Walt Disney Pictures/ Pixar Animation Studios, 2017.

Introduction

The Addams Family. New York: ABC, 1964–1966.

Anzaldúa, Gloria, and Cherrie Moraga. *This Bridge Called My Back: Writings by Radical Women of Color*. Watertown, Mass.: Persephone Press, 1981.

Aparicio, Frances, and Susana Chávez-Silverman, eds. *Tropicalizations: Transcultural Representations of Latinidad*. Hanover, NH: University Press of New England, 1997.

Bebout, Lee. *Whiteness on the Border: Mapping the U.S. Racial Imagination in Brown and White*. New York: New York University Press, 2016.

Border Wars. Washington, D.C.: National Geographic Channel, 2010–2015.

Cuarón, Alfonso, dir. *Children of Men*. Universal City, Calif.: Universal Pictures, 2006.

Cuarón, Alfonso, dir. *Y Tu Mamá Tambien*. Los Angeles, Calif.: Twentieth Century Fox, 2001.

East Willy B. Web series. http://www.eastwillyb.com/.

English, James F. *The Economy of Prestige: Prizes, Awards, and the Circulation of Cultural Value*. Cambridge, Mass.: Harvard University Press, 2008.

Fojas, Camilla. "Border Media and New Spaces of Latinidad." In *Latinos and Narrative Media: Participation and Portrayal*, edited by Frederick Luis Aldama, 35–47. New York: Palgrave Macmillan, 2013.

González Iñárritu, Alejandro, dir. *Carne y arena*. Burbank, Calif.: Legendary Entertainment, 2017.

Kerouac, Jack. *On the Road*. New York: Viking, 1957.

Martin, Darnell, dir. *I Like It Like That*. Culver City, Calif.: Columbia Pictures, 1994.

My Three Sons. ABC/CBS, 1960–1972.

Negrón-Muntaner, Frances. *Boricua Pop: Puerto Ricans and the Latinization of American Culture*. New York: New York University Press, 2004.

Nguyen, Viet Thanh. *Nothing Ever Dies: Vietnam and the Memory of War*. Cambridge, Mass.: Harvard University Press, 2016.

Ozark. Los Gatos, Calif.: Netflix, 2017–.

Ramos, Jorge. *The Latino Wave: How Hispanics Are Transforming Politics in America*. New York: Harper Perennial, 2005.

Scrubs. New York: ABC/NBC, 2001–2010.

Shepard, Dax, dir. *CHiPS*. Burbank, Calif.: Warner Bros. Pictures, 2017.

Siempre en Domingo. Mexico City: Televisa, 1969–1998.

Underworld Inc. Washington, D.C.: National Geographic, 2015.

Valdivia, Angharad N. *Latina/os and the Media*. Cambridge, U.K.: Polity Press, 2010.

Wallace, Carvell. "Why 'Black Panther' Is a Defining Moment for Black America." *New York Times*, February 12, 2018. https://www.nytimes.com/2018/02/12/magazine/why-black -panther-is-a-defining-moment-for-black-america.html.

Chapter 1

Aldama, Arturo. *Disrupting Savagism: Intersecting Chicana/o, Mexican Immigrant, and Native American Struggles for Self-Representation*. Durham, N.C.: Duke University Press, 2001.

Beltrán, Mary. *Latina/o Stars in U.S. Eyes: The Making and Meanings of Film and TV Stardom*. Urbana: University of Illinois Press, 2009.

Better Call Saul. New York: AMC, 2015–.

Breaking Bad. New York: AMC, 2008–2013.

Bukowski, Charles. "The Murder of Ramon Vasquez." In *Erections, Ejaculations and General Tales of Ordinary Madness*. San Francisco: City Lights, 1972.

Dávila, Arlene. *Latinos, Inc.: The Marketing and Making of a People*. Berkeley: University of California Press, 2001.

Fojas, Camilla. *Border Bandits: Hollywood on the Southern Frontier*. Austin: University of Texas Press, 2008.

Fregoso, Rosa Linda. *The Bronze Screen: Chicana and Chicano Film Culture*. Minneapolis: University of Minnesota Press, 1993.

Griffith, D. W., dir. *Birth of a Nation*. Hollywood, Calif.: Reliance-Majestic Studios, 1915.

Hayek, Salma. "Harvey Weinstein Is My Monster Too." *New York Times*, December 12, 2017.

Huston, John, dir. *Treasure of the Sierra Madre*. Burbank, Calif.: Warner Bros., 1948.

Jones, F. Richard, dir. *The Gaucho*. Hollywood, Calif.: United Artists, 1927.

Kazan, Elia, dir. *Viva Zapata!*. Los Angeles: Twentieth Century Fox, 1952.

Lewis, Oscar. *Children of Sanchez*. New York: Random House, 1961.

Menéndez, Ramón, dir. *Stand and Deliver*. Burbank, Calif.: Warner Bros., 1988.

Scorcese, Martin, dir. *Gangs of New York*. Los Angeles: Miramax, 2002.

Valdez, Luis, dir. *The Cisco Kid*. Atlanta: Turner Pictures, 1994.

Valdez, Luis, dir. *La Bamba*. Culver City, Calif.: Columbia Pictures, 1987.

Valdez, Luis, dir. *Zoot Suit*. Universal City, Calif.: Universal Pictures, 1981.

Wells, Orson, dir. *Touch of Evil*. Universal City, Calif.: Universal Pictures, 1958.

Chapter 2

Burke, James, writer. *Connections*. London: BBC, 1978.

Campbell, Martin, dir. *The Mask of Zorro*. Culver City, Calif.: Tristar Pictures, 1998.

Dragnet. Season 2, episode 15, "The Christmas Story." Aired December 21, 1967, on NBC.

Fregoso, Rosa Linda. *The Bronze Screen: Chicana and Chicano Film Culture*. Minneapolis: University of Minnesota Press, 1993.

Heineman, Matthew, dir. *Cartel Land*. New York: Orchard, 2015.

Hill, Walter, dir. *The Warriors*. Hollywood, Calif.: Paramount Pictures, 1979.

Homeland Security USA. ABC, 2009. https://en.wikipedia.org/wiki/Homeland_Security_USA.
Miami Vice. New York: NBC, 1984–1990.
Narcos. Los Gatos Calif.: Netflix, 2015–.
Queen of the South. Los Gatos, Calif.: 2016–.
Snyder, Zachary, dir. *Batman v Superman: Dawn of Justice*. Burbank, Calif.: Warner Bros., 2016.
Sutter, Kurt, creator. *Sons of Anarchy*. Los Angeles: FX, 2008–2015.
13 Reasons Why. Los Gatos, Calif.: Netflix, 2017.

Chapter 3

All in the Family. Hollywood, Calif.: CBS, 1971–1979.
Bonanza. New York: NBC, 1959–1973.
Brooklyn Nine-Nine. Los Angeles: Fox, 2013–.
Chico and the Man. New York: NBC, 1974–1978.
Cristela. New York: ABC, 2014–2015.
de la Peña, Adam. *Minoriteam*. Atlanta: Adult Swim, 2005–2006.
Freleng, Fritz, and Hawley Pratt, creators. "Speedy Gonzales." *Looney Tunes*. Burbank, Calif.: Warner Bros., 1953–2015.
George Lopez. New York: ABC, 2002–2007.
Gilligan's Island. New York: CBS, 1964–1967.
González, Christopher. *Permissible Narratives: The Promise of Latino/a Literature*. Columbus: Ohio State University Press, 2017.
Good Times. New York: CBS, 1974–1979.
Happy Days. New York: ABC, 1974–1984.
Hess, Jared, dir. *Nacho Libre*. Los Angeles: Nickelodeon Movies, 2006.
Hess, Jared, dir. *Napoleon Dynamite*. Hollywood, Calif.: Fox Searchlight Pictures, 2004.
I Love Lucy. New York: CBS, 1951–1957.
Louie. Los Angeles: FX, 2010–2015.
Marín, Cheech. *Born in East L.A.* Universal City, Calif.: Universal Pictures, 1987.
Mastro, Dana E., and Elizabeth Behm-Morawitz. "Latino Representation on Primetime Television." *Journalism and Mass Communication Quarterly* 82, no. 1 (2005): 110–30.
Maude. New York: CBS, 1972–1978.
Mendible, Myra, ed. *From Bananas to Buttocks: The Latina Body in Popular Film and Culture*. Austin: University of Texas Press, 2007.
Nericcio, William. *Tex[t]-Mex: Seductive Hallucinations of the "Mexican" in America*. Austin: University of Texas Press, 2007.
Niblo, Fred, dir. *Mark of Zorro*. Hollywood, Calif.: United Artists, 1920.
Noriega, Chon, and Ana M. López, eds. *The Ethnic Eye: Latino Media Arts*. Minneapolis: University of Minnesota Press, 1996.
Ovalle, Priscilla. *Dance and the Hollywood Latina: Race, Sex, and Stardom*. New Brunswick, NJ: Rutgers University Press, 2011.
Sanford and Son. New York: NBC, 1972–1977.
The High Chaparral. New York: NBC, 1967.

Chapter 4

Barney and Friends. PBS, 1992–2010.
Bordertown. Los Angeles: Fox, 2016.
Bordertown: Laredo. "The Candyman," http://www.dailymotion.com/video/x2ijxxw.
Cameron, Cody, dir. *Cloudy with a Chance of Meatballs 2*. Culver City, Calif.: Sony Pictures, 2013.

Coffin, Pierre, dir. *Despicable Me*. Universal City, Calif.: Universal Pictures, 2010.

Coffin, Pierre. *Despicable Me 2*. Universal City, Calif.: Universal Pictures, 2013.

El chapulín Colorado. Mexico City: Canal de las Estrellas, 1972–1981.

El Chavo del Ocho. Mexico City: Televisa, 1971–1980.

El Tigre: The Adventures of Manny Rivera. New York: Nickelodeon, 2007–2008.

Family Guy. Los Angeles: Fox, 1999–.

Handy Manny. Burbank, Calif.: Disney Junior, 2006–.

Lasseter, John, dir. *A Bug's Life*. Burbank, Calif.: Walt Disney Pictures; Emeryville, Calif.: Pixar Animation Studios, 1998.

Lasseter, John, dir. *Cars*. Burbank, Calif.: Walt Disney Pictures; Emeryville, Calif.: Pixar Animation Studios, 2006.

Lasseter, John, dir. *Cars 2*. Burbank, Calif.: Walt Disney Pictures; Emeryville, Calif.: Pixar Animation Studios, 2011.

Lord, Phil, dir. *Cloudy with a Chance of Meatballs*. Culver City, Calif.: Sony Pictures Animation, 2009.

Melamedoff, Michael, dir. *The Problem with Apu*. New York: TruTV, 2017.

Miller, George, dir. *Happy Feet 2*. Burbank, Calif.: Warner Bros. Pictures, 2011.

Molina-Guzmán, Isabel. *Dangerous Curves: Latina Bodies in the Media*. New York: New York University Press, 2010.

The Office. New York: NBC, 2005–2013.

The Powerpuff Girls. Atlanta: Cartoon Network, 1998–2005.

Ripoll, Maria, dir. *Tortilla Soup*. Culver City, Calif.: Samuel Goldwyn Films, 2001.

Scribner, George, dir. *Oliver and Company*. Burbank, Calif.: Walt Disney Pictures, 1988.

Sesame Street. Arlington, VA: PBS, 1969–.

Soren, David, dir. *Turbo*. Glendale, Calif.: DreamWorks Animation, 2013.

The Simpsons. Los Angeles: Fox, 1989–.

The Super Friends. Season 6, episode 6, "Alien Mummy." Aired October 1981 on ABC.

Supergirl. New York: CBS, 2015–.

Verbinski, Gore, dir. *Rango*. Los Angeles: Nickelodeon Movies, 2011.

Chapter 5

Claws. Atlanta: TNT, 2017–.

Devious Maids. Burbank, Calif.: ABC, 2013–2016.

In Living Color. Los Angeles: Fox, 1990–1994.

Jane the Virgin. Burbank, Calif.: CW, 2014–.

Los Americans. Season 1, episode 1. Web. Accessed June 11, 2017 https://www.youtube.com/watch?v=ANCS49kVUGE.

Martin, Darnell, dir. *I Like It Like That*. Culver City, Calif.: Columbia Pictures, 1994.

Modern Family. New York: ABC, 2009–.

Molina-Guzmán, Isabel. *Latinas and Latinos on TV: Colorblind Comedy in the Post-Racial Network Era*. Tucson: University of Arizona Press, 2018.

Mulvey, Laura. "Visual Pleasure and Narrative Cinema." In *Film Theory and Criticism: Introductory Readings*, edited by Leo Braudy and Marshall Cohen, 833–44. New York: Oxford University Press, 1999.

My So-Called Life. New York: ABC, 1994–1995.

Orange is the New Black. Los Gatos, Calif.: Netflix, 2013–.

Paredez, Deborah. *Selenidad: Selena, Latinos, and the Performance of Memory*. Durham, N.C.: Duke University Press, 2009.

Rodriguez, Richard T. *Next of Kin: The Family in Chicano/a Cultural Politics*. Durham, N.C.: Duke University Press, 2009.

Rojas, Theresa. "Illuminated Bodies: Kat Von D and the Borderlands of Tattoo Culture." In *Latinos and Narrative Media: Participation and Portrayal*, edited by Frederick Luis Aldama, 117–28. New York: Palgrave Macmillan, 2013.

Shades of Blue. New York: NBC, 2016–.

Silliman, Jael, Marlene Gerber Fried, Loretta Ross, and Elena R. Gutiérrez, eds. *Undivided Rights: Women of Color Organize for Reproductive Justice.* Cambridge, Mass.: South End Press, 2004.

True Blood. New York: HBO, 2008–2014.

Wang, Wayne, dir. *Maid in Manhattan.* Culver City, Calif.: Columbia Pictures, 2002.

Chapter 6

Agents of S.H.I.E.L.D Slingshot. http://abc.go.com/shows/marvels-agents-of-shield-slingshot.

Aldama, Frederick Luis. *Latinx Superheroes in Mainstream Comics.* Tucson: University of Arizona Press, 2017.

Arau, Sergio. *A Day Without a Mexican.* Hollywood, Calif.: Altavista Films, 2004.

Ayala, Diego. *Conexión.* Santiago: Azar Producciones, 2013.

Batman. New York: ABC, 1966–1968.

Battlestar Galactica. New York: ABC, 1978–1979.

Brujos. http://www.brujostv.com/.

Caprica. New York: SyFy, 2010.

Chee, Fabio. "Science Fiction in Latino Studies Today . . . and in the Future." In *The Routledge Companion to Latino/a Pop Culture*, edited by Frederick Luis Aldama, 110–19. New York: Routledge, 2016.

Dusk till Dawn: The Series. Austin, Tex.: El Rey Network, 2014–.

Edwards, Gareth, dir. *Monsters.* London: Vertigo Films, 2010.

The Event. New York: NBC, 2010–2011.

Exorcist. Los Angeles: Fox, 2016–.

The Flash. Burbank, Calif.: CW, 2014–.

Galactica 1980. New York: ABC, 1980.

González, Christopher. "Intertextploitation and Post-Post-Latinidad in *Planet Terror*." In *Critical Approaches to the Films of Robert Rodriguez*, edited by Frederick Luis Aldama, 121–39. Austin: University of Texas Press, 2015.

Kubrick, Stanley, dir. *Dr. Strangelove.* Culver City, Calif.: Columbia Pictures, 1964.

Laresgoiti, Francisco, dir. *2033.* Los Angeles, Calif.: Cinema Epoch, 2009.

Lin, Justin, dir. *Star Trek Beyond.* Hollywood, Calif.: Paramount Pictures, 2016.

Lost in Space. New York: CBS, 1965–1968.

Lucas, George, dir. *Star Wars.* San Francisco: Lucasfilm Ltd., 1977.

Meirelles, Fernando, dir. *Blindness.* Universal City, Calif.; Los Angeles: Focus Features and Miramax Films, 2008.

Ordóñez Nischli, Rodrigo, dir. *Depositarios.* Mexico City: De Cuernos Al Abismo, 2010.

Parise, Vanessa, dir. *Drink, Slay, Love.* New York: Lifetime, 2017.

Ramírez, Catherine. "Afrofuturism/Chicanafuturism: Fictive Kin." *Aztlan: A Journal of Chicano Studies* 33, no. 1 (2008): 185–94.

Ramírez Berg, Charles. *Latino Images in Film: Stereotypes, Subversion, and Resistance.* Austin: University of Texas Press, 2002.

Rivera, Alex. *A Robot Walks into a Bar.* Video, 11.57. https://www.youtube.com/watch?v=fOz1cMu7hZQ.

Rivera, Alex. "Toward a Transfrontera-LatinX Aesthetic: An Interview with Filmmaker Alex Rivera." By Frederick Aldama. *Latino Studies* 15, no. 3 (2017): 373–80.

Rivera, Alex. *Why Cybraceros?* Video, 4:51. https://www.youtube.com/watch?v=Xr1eqKcDZq4.

Rodriguez, Robert, dir. *From Dusk till Dawn*. Los Angeles: Miramax Films, 1996.

Rodriguez, Robert, dir. *Machete*. Austin, Tex.: Troublemaker Studios, 2010.

Rodriguez, Robert, dir. *Machete Kills*. Austin, Tex.: Troublemaker Studios, 2013.

Rodriguez, Robert, dir. *Planet Terror*. Austin, Tex.: Troublemaker Studios, 2007.

Rodriguez, Robert, dir. *Sleep Dealer*. Los Angeles: Maya Entertainment, 2008.

Rodriguez, Robert, dir. *Spy Kids*. New York: Dimension Films; Austin, Tex.: Troublemaker Studios, 2001.

Salces, Carlos, dir. *Zurdo*. Hollywood, Calif.: Altavista Films, 2003.

Sapir, Esteban, dir. *La antena*. Buenos Aires: Pachamama Cine, 2007.

Scott, Ridley, dir. *Blade Runner*. Burbank, Calif.: Warner Bros., 1982.

Soderbergh, Steven, dir. *Contagion*. Burbank, Calif.: Warner Bros, 2011.

Star Trek: Discovery. New York: CBS, 2017–.

Villeneuve, Denis, dir. *Blade Runner 2049*. Burbank, Calif.: Warner Bros., 2017.

The Walking Dead. New York: AMC, 2010–.

Westworld. New York: HBO, 2017–.

Wonder Woman. New York: CBS, 1975–1979.

Z Nation. New York: SyFy, 2017.

INDEX

Acosta, Oscar Zeta, 84
Adler, Lou, 78
Aguilera, Cristina, 31
Alba, Jessica, 16, 19, 53, 88, 99, 100, 127, 145, 147
Alcaraz, Lalo, 10
Alien, 68, 137
Alonzo, Cristela, 82, 84, 95
Alonso, María Conchita, 20, 34, 64
"The Ambiguously Gay Duo," 43
American Gangster, 137
American Latino Media Arts (ALMA), 14
American Me, 21, 50, 73
Annihilation, 144–45
Antal, Nimród, 141
Anthony, Marc, 129
anxiety of arrival, 14
Apocalypto, 108
Arau, Alfonso, 109
Arenas, Nathan, 103
Arias, Yancey, 71
Armageddon, 21
Arnaz, Desi, 37
Aronofsky, Darren, 27, 143
Arteta, Miguel, 49
As the Bell Rings, 98
Asociación de Empresarios Mexicanos (AEM), 4
Avatar, 24, 28, 38, 58, 120–21, 134, 143, 161
Azalea, Iggy, 88
Azaria, Hank, 97–98

Babel, 103
Back to the Future, 20
The Back-up Plan, 122
Bad Teacher, 42
Baldwin, James, 38
Ballad of Gregorio Cortez, 21
Banderas, Antonio, 37, 39, 64, 123
Bardem, Javier, 151
Barney and Friends, 98

Batman: character, 43, 62–63, 120, 137; triology, 150
Battlestar Galactica, 138–39
Beach, Adam, 142
Beasts of No Nation, 16
The Beatles, 89
Beatriz at Dinner, 49–50
Bechdel, Alison, 102
Beltran, Robert, 34, 147
A Better Life, 47–48
Bichir, Demián, 42, 48
Birdman, 15
Birth of a Nation, 38–39, 57–61, 67, 137, 149
Black, Jack, 80
Blackish, 25
Blade Runner, 20, 34, 137–38
Blade Runner 2049, 138
Blanc, Mel, 75, 93
The Blind Side, 38
Blomkamp, Neil, 48, 134–35
Blood In, Blood Out, 18, 54
Blunt, Emily, 72
The Book of Life, 92–93
"Booty," 118
Bordertown: 1935, 39; 2006, 123
Born in East LA, 20, 99
Boyega, John, 9, 24
The Brady Bunch, 54
Branagh, Kenneth, 148
Brando, Marlon, 39
Bratt, Benjamin, 16, 23, 64, 95, 150
Bratt, Peter, 4
The Breakfast Club, 20, 45
Breaking Bad, 53, 71
The Bridge, 71
The Brief Wondrous Life of Oscar Wao, 87
Bring Me the Head of Alfredo Garcia, 68
Brody, Adrian, 141
Brooks, James L., 51
brownface, 19, 38–42, 49, 61, 63, 68, 78, 80, 137, 155

Gladiator, 137
Glee, 78, 101
Go Diego Go!, 91
Gods of Egypt, 41
Gómez Bolaños, Roberto, 21–22, 91
Gomez, Isabella, 101
Gomez, Selena, 31, 98–99
Gonzales-Gonzales, José, 140
Gonzalez Gonzalez, Pedro, 139
González Iñárritu, Alejandro, 15, 103, 123
The Good, the Bad, and the Ugly, 65–66
Gotham, 151
Grauman's Chinese Theatre, 34
Gravity, 15
Greaser Act of 1855, 39
The Greaser's Gauntlet, 38–39
The Great Gatsby, 19
Grey, Jennifer, 89
Griffith, D. W., 38–39, 57–58, 75, 87
Guerrero, Aurora, 4
Guerrero, Diane, 131
Gutiérrez, Jorge, 92–93
Guzman, Luis, 94

Hackman, Gene, 67
Hamilton, 12
Handy Manny, 92
Happy Feet 2, 19, 94
Hardy, Tom, 151
Hawaii Five-O, 9
Hayek, Salma, 4, 16, 37, 41, 43, 50, 64, 103, 110, 115, 125, 127
Hayworth, Rita (Margarita Carmen Cansino), 16, 31–32, 114, 115
Hegyes, Robert, 77
Here and Now, 109
Herles, Kathleen, 93
Hernandez, Javier, 154
Hernandez, Jay, 26
Heroes, 152
Hess, Jared, 79–80
Heston, Charlton, 40, 137
Hijuelos, Oscar, 87
"Hips Don't Lie," 88
Hispanic Organization of Latin Actors (HOLA), 14
Holland, Tom, 151

Holly, Buddy, 89
Honey, 88
Hopkins, Anthony, 63, 143
Horta, Silvio, 101
Howells, William Dean, 35
Hudson, Rock, 36, 67
Hughes, John, 45
Humans, 148
Huston, John, 68

I Like It Like That, 21
I Love Dick, 102
Ice Cube, 93
ideal audience, 31, 93, 98, 122
Iglesias, Enrique, 37
Iglesias, Gabriel, 82, 103
Iglesias, Julio, 37
In Living Color, 129
In the Heights, 12
Indelicato, Mark, 46
Independence Day, 21
Inside Llewyn Davis, 27
Instructions Not Included (*No se aceptan devoluciones*), 86, 107
Interstellar, 134
Isaac, Oscar, 9–10, 27, 133, 145
IT, 16

The Jack Benny Program, 75
Jackman, Hugh, 143–44
James, Lejuan, 5
Jameson, Frederick, 135
Jane Eyre, 16
Jane the Virgin, 13–14, 24, 47, 84–85, 117, 122, 128
Jean, Wyclef, 88
Jenkins, Barry, 4, 24
Jidaigeki, 136
Jim Crow, 119
Johnson, Don, 26
Jones, Felicity, 9
Jones, Tommy Lee, 140
Judd, Ashley, 4
Jurassic Park, 21

Kahlo, Frida, 37, 125
Katz, Evan, 139

ABOUT THE AUTHORS

FREDERICK LUIS ALDAMA is Distinguished University Professor, University Distinguished Scholar, and University Distinguished Teacher at The Ohio State University. He is the author, co-author, and editor of thirty-six books, including *Long Stories Cut Short* and the Eisner Award–winner *Latinx Superheroes in Mainstream Comics*.

CHRISTOPHER GONZÁLEZ is an associate professor of English and the director of the Latinx Cultural Center at Utah State University in Logan, Utah. He is the author, co-author, and editor of numerous books, including the Perkins Prize Honorable Mention *Permissible Narratives: The Promise of Latino/a Literature*.